Children and Spirituality

of related interest

The Spirit of the Child
Revised Edition
David Hay with Rebecca Nye
ISBN 978 1 84310 371 4

Spiritual Healing with Children with Special Needs
Bob Woodward
Foreword by Dr Hugh Gayer, The Sheiling School Medical Adviser
ISBN 978 1 84310 545 9

The Challenge of Practical Theology
Selected Essays
Stephen Pattison
ISBN 978 1 84310 453 7

Spiritual Dimensions of Pastoral Care
Practical Theology in a Multidisciplinary Context
Edited by David Willows and John Swinton
Foreword by Don Browning
ISBN 978 1 85302 892 2

Young Children's Rights
Exploring Beliefs, Principles and Practice
2nd edition
Priscilla Alderson
Foreword by Mary John
ISBN 978 1 84310 599 2
Children in Charge Series 13

Children and Spirituality

Searching for Meaning
and Connectedness

Brendan Hyde

Jessica Kingsley Publishers
London and Philadelphia

First published in 2008
by Jessica Kingsley Publishers
116 Pentonville Road
London N1 9JB, UK
and
400 Market Street, Suite 400
Philadelphia, PA 19106, USA

www.jkp.com

Library of Congress Cataloging in Publication Data
Hyde, Brendan.
    Children and spirituality : searching for meaning and connectedness / Brendan Hyde.
        p. cm.
    Includes bibliographical references (p.   ).
    ISBN-13: 978-1-84310-589-3 (pb : alk. paper) 1. Children--Religious life. 2. Religious
education of children. I. Title.
    BL625.5.H925 2008
    204.083--dc22

                                                                            2007033182

British Library Cataloguing in Publication Data
A CIP catalogue record for this book is available from the British Library

ISBN 978 1 84310 589 3

Contents

Acknowledgements

There are many people who need to be acknowledged as having being influential in my own thinking and who have, in one way or another, contributed to the writing of this book. I would like to especially thank my colleagues at Australian Catholic University – Kath Engebretson, Richard Rymarz and Michael Buchanan – for their encouragement and critical dialogue. I would especially like to thank Marian de Souza, who has been my mentor, and who has opened me to my own sense of spirituality. I would also like to acknowledge and thank my colleagues from the International Association of Children's Spirituality, particularly Cathy Ota, Clive and Jane Erricker, as well as other colleagues from Britain – Kate Adams, Richard Woolley, Tony Eaude and Mark Chater, who have at various stages, and in different ways, affirmed my work. I would also like to thank Tobin Hart for his inspiration and encouragement.

My appreciation must also be expressed to the staff at Jessica Kingsley Publishers, especially Jessica Stevens and Lucy Mitchell, who showed a genuine interest in my work, and an eagerness to take it on. I am most grateful.

To the children who participated in the research which led to the writing of this book I am most grateful. Their generosity of time and willingness to share aspects of their inner lives enabled me to learn extensively about their spirituality. Without their participation, my study, and hence this book, would not have come to fruition.

In particular, I would like acknowledge the support of my family – my wife, Martine, and children Christopher and Thomas – for their extreme patience, encouragement and good humour. I would especially like to thank Thomas for showing and reminding his daddy of what it means to experience wonder and awe, and to engage in the here and now of my own experience.

Finally, for my own mum and dad, whose presence I have never ceased to experience and whose guidance has continued to drive me in unexplainable ways. This work is for you.

Preface

The spirituality of children has gained much attention in recent times, particularly in Western culture. The reasons for this have been many and varied. They include educational concerns for the development of the whole child, building resilience against depression, drug and alcohol abuse, and youth suicide, an interest in bolstering the voice of the child (often associated with the rights of the child), and a desire to better understand the world of the child – a world which is perceived to be quite different from the world of the adult. In many cases these concerns are not explicitly labelled as children's spirituality, but are disguised beneath other issues – the notion of well being, promoting values education, children's development, initiatives such as *Every Child Matters*, and the like. Whatever the reasons or guises, children's spirituality has captured the interest of those who work and engage with children in a variety of capacities – teachers, early childhood specialists, counsellors, youth workers, and of course, and perhaps most importantly, parents.

Accompanying this interest and attention, a growing body of research is being established in relation to children's spirituality. Today, this field of research is multidisciplinary, and includes the specializations of psychology, education, philosophy, neuroscience, theology, and even medicine. There is an international association for children's spirituality, of which many who work in the above fields are members, and several other institutes which focus on the spiritual dimension of children's lives, including the ChildSpirit Institute in Georgia, Atlanta. There are also regular conferences which focus on the theme of children's spirituality, including the international conferences on children's spirituality, which emanated originally in Britain but which are now hosted by a variety of countries worldwide.

However, while much research has taken place and has provided valuable insight into the spiritual dimension of children's lives, there is still much to be done, and many questions continue to arise. What does children's spirituality look like? How might adults who work with, or who parent children, recognize the spirituality of children when they encounter it? What should they do about it? How should they nurture it?

All of this serves to demonstrate the growing popularity that the field of children's spirituality currently enjoys. It also presents something of a background, or context, out of which my own research in this area has emanated, and of the types of questions I have raised myself, which ultimately has led to my writing of this book. My concern in this work is to provide those who engage with children in various capacities – teachers, early childhood specialists, counsellors, and parents – something tangible in terms of what to be alert for in recognizing the characteristics of children's spirituality. In being able to recognize it, it is my hope that those who engage with children might be able to nurture it.

In writing this book I have attempted, for the most part, to avoid unnecessary jargon, and to utilize a style accessible to readers coming to this text from the various backgrounds mentioned above. Guidelines have been provided in the chapters comprising the second section of this book for nurturing the various characteristics of children's spirituality that have been identified through my own investigation.

I offer *Children and Spirituality* as a guide and resource for teachers and parents, and for others who may work and engage with children in various capacities.

PART 1
Preparing the Ground

CHAPTER 1

Introduction

The field of children's spirituality is a relatively new area of exploration. While it has certainly gained momentum and popularity in recent times, many questions continue to abound. What does the spirituality of children look like? How do adults – parents, teachers, and others who work and interact with children – know when children are expressing their spirituality? And when children do express their spirituality, what should adults do? How might they nurture it? By way of introduction, the following five short vignettes[1] may provide some clues as to the direction this book will take in exploring children's spirituality:

Playing in the park...
It is a sunny afternoon in springtime, and David is playing on the swing in the local park. His dad is pushing him, and the rhythm of the swing moving back and forth leads David to close his eyes. As the swing is gradually pushed higher and higher, David begins to giggle. He can feel the rush of wind against his face and the giddy sensation in his tummy as the swing gains momentum in moving backwards and forwards in constant rhythm. He is aware of his bodily movement and of his own physicality – his hands clutching the chain of the swing, his bottom on the seat, and his legs stretched out as the swing propels forwards, and tucked underneath as the swing retreats backwards. He has a deep-down feeling of contentment. At this moment, nothing else matters to David. He is attending to the here and now of his experience. There is no past. There is no future. Just the present moment in which he is situated.

The inquisitive philosopher...
Jane is three years old. Her family is having dinner together one evening and is chatting about some of the antics that Michael – Jane's older brother who is now nine years old – got up to when he was a youngster. Jane listens intently as her mother recounts the time Michael was playing in the backyard and got himself stuck in the branch of the large elm tree. All of the members of the family laugh heartily. Jane is hanging on every

word that her mother says. She seems to be captivated by this story. When the laughing has subsided, Jane turns to her mother and asks, 'Where was I when Michael got stuck in the tree?' Jane's mother looks lovingly at her and replies, 'You weren't born then, sweetheart.' But Jane's wonder and curiosity have been aroused, and she has a sense of connection to something greater. Insistently, she pursues the conversation. 'Yes, I know,' persists Jane, 'but, *where was I?*'

Showing empathy...

Tam is playing happily on the adventure playground equipment at kindergarten. As the other children finish their games and get ready to go inside for some quiet time, Tam notices that one little boy named George is trying to reach the tap at the drinking fountain. But being a short little fellow, his mouth cannot quite reach the spout. Having been in that situation before, Tam empathizes with George. She knows how frustrating that can be, especially when you are so thirsty. She watches George for a few moments, and then sees her kindergarten teacher coming towards her. 'Are you coming inside, Tam?' asks her teacher. 'Yes,' replies Tam, 'but I think I should get a small chair for George to stand on. He can't reach the tap to get a drink.'

Making sense of the death of a pet...

Jake's pet dog, Scamper, died last week. It was an emotional time for Jake and his two sisters, but he seems to be coping well at the moment. Today, Jake has a friend over to play, and his father listens as Jake describes to his friend how they buried Scamper in the back garden. 'I was really sad,' begins Jake. 'My dad dug a hole and we buried him near the big tree near the back fence. But this week, I don't feel quite as sad. I saw this show on TV where a mother died right after she had her baby. The bloke who was the dad said he couldn't believe how the baby looked just like the mother. He even said that he thought the baby *was* the mum, come back to life. Now, the lady down the street has a dog that has just had pups. They were born right around the time that Scamper died. I think that maybe Scamper's spirit is sort of alive in one of those baby pups...one of them even looks a bit like Scamper...' Jake's dad is amazed. They were not really a religious family. So, where had he learnt about things like spirits, and what seemed like a form of reincarnation? And how on earth was he able to make sense of the loss of a family pet in that particular way?

Seeing the invisible...

Lisa is nine years old. Ever since she can remember, she has been able to see lights that seem to shine around people. Although she does not have the language to name them, they are called auras. Lisa sees them quite naturally, and assumes that other people can see them too. One day, she is walking with her mother, and sees a magnificent aura around a gentleman who is walking towards them. She smiles politely as the gentleman walks past. He smiles politely in return. 'Did you see that?' asks Lisa. 'That man has a beautiful light around him, doesn't he.' Her mother turns to look at her. 'What are you talking about darling?' she asks. 'The light…around the man we just passed. Look…' she says pointing towards him. 'Perhaps you mean the reflection of the sun…' begins her mother. 'No,' says Lisa, 'I mean the light around him, like the light around you.' Lisa's mother doesn't know quite how to respond. Lisa has never said anything like this before, and it is a little unsettling. 'Sweetheart,' begins her mother, 'people don't have lights around them. You must be mistaking it for the reflection of the sun.' Lisa's mother pauses in thought for a moment. 'Perhaps it's best if you don't tell other people things like this,' she continues cautiously. 'They might not understand…and they might think that there is something not quite normal…'

Lisa is confused. She has always seen auras around people. The sudden realization that other people do not necessarily see them leaves her feeling ill at ease. 'There is nothing wrong with me,' she thinks. 'I thought everyone could see them.'

In each of the instances above, the children were revealing something of their spiritual lives. For the most part, their spirituality was being revealed in the ordinary events and activities of childhood – playing at the park, asking inquisitive and perhaps existential questions, making sense of an event, and in seeing someone in need of a helping hand. These experiences, and others like them, are everyday occurrences which abound in the lives of children. If adults are alert to them, they could be gaining a window into children's spiritual lives. In some instances too, children's spirituality is revealed in relation to their experience of the more subtle levels of reality, such as perceiving energy around people, hearing voices or perhaps seeing visions. Some children are able to tune into these intuitive capacities, and these types of experiences are more common than many believe. This can be challenging for adults, especially for parents who may fear and perceive that their child may be, in some way, abnormal, perhaps even psychotic.

The gradual awareness in recent times that activities such as those detailed above, and many others besides, could be experienced by some children as spiritual has led to an increasing body of research in the field of children's spirituality, and a general interest in this area on the part of many adults.

A Growing Interest in Children's Spirituality

There are a number of more specific factors which have led to a growing interest in children's spirituality, particularly in countries such as England, the United States of America, Australia and New Zealand. For example, in England and Wales, measures have been taken to ensure that spirituality is addressed within the curriculum of both primary and secondary education in both state and church related settings. This emanated from the British 1944 Education Act and has been reinforced more recently in various education documents. The National Curriculum Council released a document titled *Spiritual and Moral Development* (1993) stressing the need for schools to include spiritual education as an integral part of the curriculum. Similarly, the Office for Standards in Education (Ofsted, 1994) produced in its handbook a statement indicating that all areas of the curriculum ought to contribute to the spiritual development of students. Following this, numerous scholars working within the British context have sought to clarify and identify the ways in which spiritual education might occur in the educational curriculum (for example, Broadbent 2004; Cottingham 2005; Kibble 2003; Watson 2003).

In countries such as the United States of America, a focus on the spiritual dimension has occurred through the notion of holistic development, where education is envisaged not just in terms of a transmission of knowledge but is also inclusive of other non-cognitive dimensions of learning. Tobin Hart, founder of the ChildSpirit Institute in Georgia, Atlanta, has extended the notion of children's spirituality beyond the classroom environment. He has proposed a spiritual programme underpinned by ten principles for use by parents and caregivers (Hart 2003). They include the child finding a voice, mastering the self, seeing a future, and listening with the heart. These principles provide ways of empowering the spirituality of children. They are not specific to any one religious tradition, but transect the deep structures of human life, and provide touchstones for parents and those who engage with children.

In countries such as Australia and New Zealand, an interest in spirituality has arisen more generally in terms of the well being and resilience of children and young people. In these countries, factors such as youth suicide, an increase in drug and alcohol abuse, combined with an escalation in delinquency, have impacted negatively on well being. It has been demonstrated that a sense of connectedness with family and the wider community can act as a protective factor and as a means by which to build resilience in young people (see for example Eckersley 1998, 2005). The notion of connectedness, as we shall see, is closely associated with spirituality.

Another factor that has led to an interest in children's spirituality is the environment in which children in developed countries grow up. In outlining her notion of toxic childhood syndrome, British writer and broadcaster Sue Palmer describes those features of the present environment which may serve to contaminate the world of children – the food they eat, their sleeping habits, the influence of electronic media (including television, mobile telephones), and the pace of life in a capitalist culture, to name but a few. This has often led to the need for children to draw on their own inner strength and inner resources to survive in an environment which, on the one hand, furnishes children with the bounties of life in a global village (fast food, computer games, the internet, and the like) while, on the other hand, it ignores their need for unconditional love and their inherent worth as human beings. Parents and those who work with children in various capacities have sought ways to counteract this environment, and to nurture the inner lives of children. The notion of an inner life is also closely associated with spirituality.

My own interest in children's spirituality came initially from my work with children and teachers in the Catholic primary school system. Like many other educators in that system, I began to question how Catholic schools could nurture the spirituality of students using curriculum materials that appeared to take little account of the realities of children's lives, and which showed, at best, a very narrow and limited understanding of the ways in which children make meaning and formulate their worldviews. The act of meaning-making is another concept closely associated with spirituality. It concerned me also that in my experience of Catholic schools there was much talk about the importance of the spiritual life generally, yet nobody seemed to be able to articulate or describe what was meant by spirituality. It was a vague term that seemed to be used interchangeably with religion. This didn't sit comfortably with me. I knew that spirituality was a much broader concept than religion. As a teacher, many of the children I had taught often had little or no contact with formal religion, yet I would have described some of these children as being deeply spiritual.

As I began my career as an academic, I was fortunate enough to have been steered in the direction of Hay and Nye's seminal work *The Spirit of the Child* (2006). These two scholars sought to develop a theoretical framework or an interpretation of children's spirituality based on the reflections of what the children themselves said in conversation with the field worker, Rebecca Nye. Importantly, their study attempted to reflect the reality of the Western world into which these children had been socialized. While aware of the divide that has grown between spirituality and traditional religion, Hay and Nye explored ways in which the spiritual life of children could be recognized in the absence of traditional religious images and language. Their work provided me with the initial impetus and inspiration for devising my research project which would explore specifically the features, or characteristics, of children's spirituality so that adults who work with children might be able to recognize children's spirituality when they encountered it, and in recognizing it, they might also be able to nurture it.

My Investigation

The investigation reported in this book then details an account of my own research into children's spirituality. Originally, my study was focused largely on children attending Catholic primary schools, and on providing recommendations for those who taught in that particular sector. However, since completing my investigation, I have been in the privileged position of being able to reflect further on the findings of my study, as well as being able to engage in critical discussion with my university colleagues in relation to the findings and implications of my investigation. As a result, I am now able to see larger connections and implications in relation to the characteristics I have identified. Not only are they significant for educators, but they also have great relevance for parents and others who work with, or who have an interest in children's spirituality, especially in Western culture. Therefore, my aim in writing this book is threefold:

1. to offer a description of spirituality and how it was understood in my own research

2. to present and discuss the characteristics of children's spirituality which I have identified through conversation with and observations of small groups of children

3. to propose some guidelines for teachers, parents, and others who work with children in various capacities, in relation to how the spirituality of children may be nurtured in the light of the identified characteristics.

There are two influencing factors which I need to reveal at this point. The first concerns the setting of my research. My study was conducted in Australia and the participants comprised children in Australian Catholic primary schools. The key reason for this was that, not only was I working at a university which had close affiliations with Catholic schools through its professional practice programme for undergraduate students, but also the Catholic Education

Office in Melbourne was very supportive of the study and interested in the findings of the investigation in terms of how they might impact on Catholic schools. However, Australia is a secular country and is typical of many other Western cultures. The findings of my research, although emanating from an Australian context, are applicable to other Westernized and developed countries. While my study was limited to some children in Catholic schools, and not designed to make broad generalizations (as will be discussed in Chapter 4), the findings were consistent with, and reflect the results of other studies which have explored the spirituality of children in other Western countries and in other educational settings (for example, Champagne 2003; Erricker, Erricker, Sullivan, Ota and Fletcher 1997; Hart 2003; Hay and Nye 2006; Moriarty 2007). In other words, the findings of my research are trustworthy and have implications for children in a range of Western countries and in a range of settings.

The second concerns my own Christian background and my extensive and significant experience in teaching, planning, and curriculum development in education in Catholic primary schools. This is recognized and made explicit here at the beginning of this book. While I have made every effort not to allow personal judgments, values and theoretical inclinations to overtly influence the content of this book, it is acknowledged that absolute objectivity on the part of a researcher is impossible (as is also discussed in Chapter 4). Accordingly, my confessional position is here made explicit.

Why Children's Spirituality is Important

The short vignettes at the beginning of this chapter attest to the spiritual dimension of children's lives through the ordinary events of childhood, and, in some instances, through their experiences of the more subtle levels of reality. These experiences are important. Spiritual awareness underpins altruistic and ethical behaviour, as can be seen in Tam's empathy for George who cannot reach the tap to get a drink. She suggests that she should get a chair on which he could stand to reach the spout. In swinging on the swing, David effactually experiences a sense of well being. Also, in his awareness of his own bodily experience on the swing, he may be using his body as a primal way of knowing, and he may experience a sense of oneness with the activity of swinging. These notions will be discussed in Chapter 5. As the inquisitive young philosopher, Jane, who wants to know where she was before she was born, is asking an existential question. She is addressing a sense of meaning and value in her own life. She is being a spiritual quester, a notion that will be elaborated upon in Chapter 8. In attempting to make sense of the death of a family pet, Jake weaves together the threads of meaning from what he has seen on television and from what he has observed in his own lived experience into a worldview which holds meaning for him, a concept that will be elaborated upon in Chapter 7. And, unless Lisa is affirmed in her capacity to see auras around people, she will suppress this feature of her life that might have enabled her to experience a sense of connectedness with others, and she will grow and develop unable to integrate this ability into her own being. A number of researchers have indicated the important role that adults play in the lives of children like Lisa. While some children are able to integrate and be nurtured by their experiences on their own, many, like Lisa, may require support and encouragement from the significant adults in their lives. Such children need adults who demonstrate a capacity to listen and who model their experience by telling their own stories, or who may make an effort to recover their own lost moments of spiritual experience (Hart 2003; Scott 2004).

In short, the types of experiences described in the five vignettes, and many others besides, need to be nurtured if children are to grow into holistic people who are developed not only cognitively, but also socially, emotionally and spiritually. In an environment in so-called developed countries which has been described as toxic (Palmer 2007), such experiences are often not nurtured and affirmed. It is not that parents and teachers are not interested and deliberately ignore them. It is just that in the daily business of secular life, they either do not have time to notice them – which is an unnaturally learned coping-with-business type of behaviour – or they do not know *what* it is they should be looking for and, when and if they do see it, they do not know *how* to nurture it.

However, the good news, to which my research, and hence this book testifies, is that the types of experience presented in each of the five vignettes at the beginning of this chapter are common experiences in childhood, including the capacity to tune into the more subtle levels of reality. Children clearly possess a rich spiritual dimension to their lives which can be nurtured if those who spend time with them are alert to the particular characteristics and features that comprise their spirituality. This book attempts to describe some of the characteristics of children's spirituality. It aims to provide adults who spend time with, and who work with children, something tangible in terms of recognizing children's expression of their spirituality. In recognizing this feature of children's lives, it then provides some suggestions and guidelines for them in nurturing the spirituality of the children with whom they are engaged.

The Organisation of this Book

The chapters of this book have been divided into two sections. Part One is titled *Preparing the Ground*, and provides a background to my study. In drawing on the literature from a number of different strands, Chapter 2 presents a conceptual understanding of spirituality, exploring and describing it from a number of different perspectives. These include religious, biological and neuro-scientific, sociological, and some psychological perspectives, the latter of which explores the notions of consciousness and Self in relation to spirituality. As a result of this, three descriptions of spirituality are offered which indicate my understanding of this term, and how its usage is to be understood throughout this book.

The third chapter examines some of the pertinent research that has taken place in the growing field of children's spirituality. The research explored emanates from a number of different Western countries including Britain, Canada, and the United States of America. It shows that while early studies in this field tended to assume that spirituality was expressed through traditional religious language and concepts, more recent investigations have utilized the perceptions, awarenesses and responses of children to ordinary everyday activities in gaining insight into their spirituality. Each of these research studies has, to greater or lesser degrees, influenced the development of my own investigation into children's spirituality.

Chapter 4 outlines the approach I used in my research for gaining insight into the spirituality of children. It describes hermeneutic phenomenology as the theoretical perspective for my study, and describes some of the practical details in terms of how the research was conducted. In keeping with the hermeneutic phenomenological tradition, I have tried, where possible, to use terms which reflect the qualitative nature of the study, rather than terms which may carry positivistic overtones.

Part Two is titled *The Characteristics of Children's Spirituality*, and each of chapters 5, 6, 7, and 8 present one of the four characteristics of children's spirituality that I identified as well as a discussion and reflection on each of those characteristics. At the conclusion of each of these chapters, some guidelines are presented for parents and those who work with children for nurturing each particular characteristic of children's spirituality. Chapter 9 discusses and reflects upon an additional feature that emerged through my research. This was the identification of two factors which appeared to inhibit the children's expression of their spirituality. This chapter also concludes with some guidelines for parents and others who work with children for counteracting these factors, which acted in a destructive way upon the children's spirituality.

The final chapter begins by suggesting some general recommendations for nurturing the spiritual dimension of children's lives. The themes of space, time, body and relationships are used as a means by which to discuss these general recommendations, and by which to draw together the threads of the discussion of the previous chapters. Following this, I briefly outline a possible pedagogical framework for nurturing spirituality in the classroom context. This is important for teachers who take seriously the education of the whole child – cognitively, socially, emotionally and spiritually. The chapter then addresses some continuing issues which may remain a concern for some readers, particularly the notion of relativism as it pertains to two of the characteristics of children's spirituality that have been revealed in my research.

CHAPTER 2

Mapping the Terrain

There are many ways in which the word spirituality may be understood. It is a term that has come to mean different things to different people. For example, spirituality has been described as pertaining to interior life, religious experience, the search for meaning and purpose, expressions of relatedness, transcendence, immanence, ultimate values, integrity, identity, connection to something greater, awareness. It has also come to be understood in relation to the 'new age' movement. All of this indicates that the term 'spirituality' has been used in various contexts with a multiplicity of diverse meanings.[2] The purpose of this chapter is to map the terrain. It describes, as the result of searching and reviewing the literature in this field, my understanding of spirituality, and the understanding that will be drawn upon throughout this book.

The notion of describing rather than defining spirituality is important. Problems in attempting to limit an understanding of spirituality to any one fixed definition have been well attested to by many writers precisely because this term can mean different things to different people (Eaude 2003). However, while spirituality may not be able to be succinctly defined, some writers, such as the British scholar Jack Priestly, argue that it can be described. Rather than attempting to limit the concept of spirituality to a single fixed definition, this chapter explores and describes spirituality from three broad perspectives – the relationship between spirituality and institutional Christianity, spirituality as a natural human predisposition, and the Divine at the core of Self, and of all existence, which connects Self with Other. These are investigated in order to tease out an understanding of the word spirituality as it is to be understood in the context of this book. As a result, I suggest that rather than being the exclusive property of any one religious tradition, spirituality is an essential human trait, that it concerns a journey towards what Australian scholar Marian de Souza has described as the notion of Ultimate Unity, and that it is given expression in terms of how one might act in relation to the human and nonhuman world.

The Relationship between Spirituality and Institutional Christianity

For many years, the word spirituality was used in Western culture principally with religious connotations. For instance, Rossiter (2005) has noted that the use of the word spirituality was once to be understood in relation to Christian religious practice, and that if one were to speak about Catholic spirituality, it was in relation to the spiritual life of religious orders, or lay members of the Church striving to emulate aspects of the life of religious orders. Traditionally understood within Christianity, spirituality drew on scripture and theology, and it was evident in people's religious practices. So connected with religion was spirituality that O'Murchu (1997) and Tacey (2000) have posited that institutional Christianity has, to a large extent, claimed ownership of spirituality, and has sought to control it, arguing it to be impossible that spiritual feelings or values could arise apart from the context of formal Christian beliefs. Drane (2000) has affirmed this, noting that in many instances, institutional Christianity has sought to contain spirituality ecclesiastically through the use of doctrine, but also through lay ministries by limiting those who could be assigned them.

However, some contemporary perspectives maintain that it is possible for spirituality to exist and to be given expression outside of any religious tradition. For instance, Tacey (2000), while not undermining the value of religion, has argued that in spite of its efforts to control spirituality, institutional Christianity is no longer able to contain it. Many people today are searching for and giving expression to their spirituality outside of formal systems of values and beliefs. In light of such an argument, different academic disciplines have argued it to be erroneous to describe spirituality as being the exclusive property of any one particular religious tradition, and that there is, in fact, a clear distinction between spirituality and institutional religion.

Spirituality is much larger and older than any form of organized formal religion. Irish scholar and social psychologist Diarmuid O'Murchu has argued that the spiritual history of the human species is at least 70,000 years old, by comparison with which, formal, organized religions have been in existence for only 4,500 years. While formal religion encompasses the organized structures, rituals and beliefs belonging to the official religious systems (Hinduism, Buddhism, Judaism, Christianity, Islam, Sikhism), spirituality concerns that 'ancient and primal search for meaning that is as old as humanity itself …and…belongs to the evolutionary unfolding of creation itself' (O'Murchu 1997, p.vii).

It was William James, the Harvard psychologist who, in *The Varieties of Religious Experience*, distinguished between institutional religion and the primordial religious experience, today more commonly known as spiritual experience. In describing religious experience, James's (1977, first published 1902) interest was not so much in institutional religion as in the original experiences that have subsequently resulted in formal religion. His concern with religion was, in essence, with the psychological experience of the individual. That is to say, James considered spirituality, or spiritual experience to be the primordial religious experience of the individual. Institutional religion becomes, then, a secondary phenomenon – a response to the original spiritual experience of the individual or community. Other more recent scholars, including Tacey (2000, 2003) and Zohar and Marshall (2000), have also understood spirituality to be the primary religious experience of the individual, and institutional religion to be the secondary phenomenon, 'the codification and communication of [the] original mystic experience or revelation...to the mass of human beings in general' (Maslow 1970a, p.19).

Importantly, Tacey (2003) has noted that although formal religion is a secondary phenomenon, a response to the original spiritual experience, this does not render it of less meaning or value. That which comes first – the spiritual – does not necessarily imply that it is better than what later ensues. Tacey argues that the initial spiritual experience can be individualistic, unrefined, and often lacking in wisdom. Because it is often idiosyncratic, the primary experience tends to be removed from the communal context, whereas the secondary development (formal religion) enables the primordial to be experienced within such a milieu. It ought to be possible to state that spirituality is the primary category, without implying that religion is therefore 'merely' secondary.

Although religion and spirituality are not synonymous, some have argued that a person's spirituality may be given expression through an organized religious belief system. For instance, Ranson (2002) has suggested that a religious tradition, such as Catholicism, may provide the context and shared value system needed to give depth and give voice to an individual's spiritual experience. Ranson maintained that spirituality comprises an arrangement of interrelated activities within two foundational moments. The first is the 'spiritual', whereby one attends and inquires into the spiritual experience which has been apperceived. The second is the 'religious', whereby one interprets and acts upon the spiritual experience, placing it into the social and communal reality, that is, into a system of shared beliefs and values (institutional religion). These two moments are held together in creative tension. Without the religious, Ranson argues, the spiritual cannot attain its depth. Yet without the spiritual, religion can present as doctrinaire.

The activities comprising these two movements are cyclical in nature. The more one attends to and inquires into their initial spiritual experience, the more one will be led to interpret and act upon it, which in turn leads one to attend, inquire and reflect upon the original experience, and so forth.

However, Ranson's construct could be considered problematic as it seems to suggest that an individual's spiritual development is incomplete unless it proceeds to the activities of interpreting and acting within an organized system of values and beliefs. To be precise, such a view in fact considers spirituality to be dependent upon formal religion, deeming institutional religion to be the larger sphere in which an individual's spirituality might be nurtured. Such an understanding has been expressed and advanced by some scholars including Wright (2000, 2004), and Carr (1995), who have rejected approaches to spirituality that do not begin with the religion. Thatcher (1996, 1999) has maintained that to speak of spirituality outside of a mainstream religious tradition is meaningless, arguing that any articulation of spirituality requires first and mostly, a theology. He has remained suspicious of so called secular and modernist treatments of spirituality that have broken 'the conceptual connection between spirituality and belief in God' (Thatcher 1996, p.122).

However, it could be argued that Thatcher's position is essentially exclusivist. His argument fails to recognize that there are many people who are not associated with any religious tradition, yet would describe themselves as spiritual. One cannot dismiss their spirituality on the grounds that they are not religious, or that they may not possess a theology to articulate it (see also Meehan 2002).

Further, some have argued that the ability to use a theology in order to articulate spirituality is a secondary and more recent phenomenon. As discussed, the spiritual history of the human species is at least 70,000 years old, by comparison with which formal, organized religions have been in existence for a mere 4,500 years. In other words, for at least some 65,000 years, the human species has neither had nor needed a theology to articulate its spirituality. Theology developed with the emergence of organized religion. For the greater part of human existence, formal religion has not existed. The spirituality of humankind was not articulated via the use of any theology.

Also, Berryman (2001) has presented the case for the non-verbal nature of spirituality. He argued that although it is difficult to define, people readily recognize spirituality when they encounter it because it is a part of humankind's non-verbal communication system. Although Berryman places emphasis on the importance of guiding people (especially children) from non-verbal spirituality into religious language as a means of nurturing spirituality, he has warned that any religious language, uprooted from its non-verbal source, is potentially destructive.

So, while institutional Christianity may have provided one possible avenue for the expression of spirituality, it is certainly not the only avenue. Spirituality cannot be contained or confined to Christianity. It is possible to apperceive spirituality outside of institutional religion.

Spiritual Experience and Institutional Religion

Supporting the notion that spirituality can exist outside of a mainstream religious tradition such as Christianity, scholarly literature suggests that there have been numerous individuals who have apperceived spiritual experience. Such individuals would include those connected with formal traditions, such as Buddhist monks who have experienced the state of *anatta*, where the self ceases to exist as a distinct and separate entity. Also, Christian mystics including Francis of Assisi, St Teresa of Jesus and Hildegard of Bingen have claimed to have experienced the presence of God as the ground of their own being. However, such spiritual experiences are not confined to the mystics and practitioners of various religious traditions. The literature indicates that all people, whether or not they belong to or practise any particular religious code, are capable of apperceiving spiritual experience.

From a psychological perspective, William James was among the first to propose that what he called 'personal religion', or spirituality as it is more commonly known today, is experienced by numerous people in a wide variety of ways, and may be used by the individual as a means to find solutions to problems of value and meaning in life. He argued that logical reason alone could not explain the religious or spiritual experience of the individual. Like other affective experiences, spiritual experience adds to life an enchantment not rationally deducible from anything else. For this reason, spirituality was considered a quality of life which provided a person with a unique sphere of power.

According to James (1977), this new sphere of power enabled an individual to draw upon her or his spiritual experiences as a mechanism for confronting and finding solutions to the difficulties and problems of life. Those who experience such mystical states apperceive them as states of absolute knowledge. They provide insight into the depths of truth unplumbed by the discursive intellect.

They are revelations, full of significance and importance. As well, they carry with them a curious and lasting sense of authority.

In his book *The Varieties of Religious Experience*, James provided an assortment of accounts in which an individual had undergone a spiritual or mystical experience, and had gone on to use this as a catalyst for living life in a particular way. The fact that there are varieties cannot be understated. No two people apperceive the same religious (spiritual) experience. They are private and individual. They function so as to lead people to act upon them and seek solutions to problems in different ways according to their life situations.

More recently, psychologist Abraham Maslow also recognized the validity of an individual's religious (spiritual) experience, arguing that it was a rightful subject for scientific investigation. He coined the phrase 'peak experiences' to describe these revelations, or mystical illuminations. While he maintained that they are common to all, or almost all people, Maslow (1970a) recognized that many people repress or suppress such experiences, and so do not use them as a source of personal therapy, growth, or fulfillment.

Further to this, Edward Robinson's study at the Religious Experience Research Unit in Oxford discovered and reported that spiritual experiences are common to a significant number of people. An extensive body of correspondence had been built up in relation to particular experiences of people, in which they felt that their lives had been affected by some power beyond themselves. Robinson (1977) noticed that a substantial proportion written by adults, described profound experiences from childhood. The experiences detailed by the participants were portrayed as being revelatory, and often affected the individual's outlook on life. These experiences from childhood had remained vivid memories of the correspondents for their whole life, and held great significance for them when contemplating questions relating to identity and meaning. While these accounts may have become embellished over time, Robinson argued that it was difficult to ignore the impact of these experiences, which in some way generated reflection in the individual.

Zohar and Marshall (2000) maintain that experiences like these, whether explicitly religious in content or otherwise, are quite common. They claim that in Western cultures, between 30 per cent and 40 per cent of the population are recorded as having undergone such experiences on at least one occasion. These types of experiences were described by those who had apperceived them as being accompanied by feelings of great euphoria and well being, and often resulted in a new perspective on life. Similarly, the American psychologist Tobin Hart reported that his research indicates that up to 80 per cent of participants (mostly adults) said that they had had a spiritual experience, and that between 60 per cent and 90 per cent of those pointed out that experiences of this nature occurred during childhood. This is significant because it suggests that children may have particular spiritual capacities and experiences which are uncommon to many adults. Hart (2003) maintained that this may be due to the openness of children to such capacities and experiences as opposed to many adults, who tend to approach the spiritual from rational thinking. Hart has maintained that spirituality lies beyond the rational, and that it is to be found in a person's inner wisdom, sense of compassion and deep meaning. All people have these spiritual capacities, although it seems that perhaps children may be more open to them.

All of this suggests that, although individuals may draw upon a religious tradition to give expression to their spirituality, they may also convey their spirituality outside of institutional religion. While in many instances institutional religion appears to have claimed ownership of spirituality, there are many people who do not practise any particular religion who have apperceived spiritual experience. This would suggest that spirituality may be accessible to all people irrespective of their membership of any particular religious tradition. In other words, spirituality may be considered to be a natural human predisposition, or an innate human trait.

Spirituality as a Natural Human Predisposition

Following on from the above discussion, there is reason to examine spirituality as an ontological reality for human beings. For instance, O'Murchu (1997) has maintained that spirituality is a natural human predisposition. It is something that people are born with, essentially dynamic and which continually seeks articulation and expression in human life. Groome (1998) has argued that spirituality is a human universal. Spirituality belongs to every person's being. It is more accurate to 'call ourselves spiritual beings who have a human life than human beings who have a spiritual life' (p.332). Similarly, Hart (2003) believes that instead of thinking of ourselves as human beings who may occasionally have spiritual experiences, it is more helpful to consider ourselves as spiritual beings who have human experiences. In writing from a Christian perspective, Rolheiser (1998) understands spirituality as something that issues forth 'from the bread and butter of ordinary life...something vital and non-negotiable lying at the heart of our lives' (p.6). Similarly, Canadian scholar Elaine Champagne argued that the human cannot be separated from the spiritual. Spirituality then can be understood to be rooted in the reality that human beings are incarnated. That is to say, people embody their spirituality. It cannot be dissociated either from the human, or from that which is beyond the human, in transcendence and in immanence.

As an ontological reality, spirituality has also been understood to be holistic in nature. British researchers David Hay and Rebecca Nye have maintained that spirituality involves a deep awareness of the whole – of one's relationship with Self and with everything that is Other than Self. Moffett (1994) has similarly written of the holistic nature of spirituality, maintaining that to be spiritual is to perceive oneness with everyone and everything and to act on this perception.

Likewise, Priestley (2002) has maintained that the spiritual is holistic. People live in a society that tends to fragment reality, and which constantly demands of people that they separate out the entities of which both individuals and groups are composed. As a necessary corrective to such a separation, Priestley has argued that a concern for the spiritual requires people to regard others as whole beings and to respond to them, each with her or his own sense of wholeness.

Zohar and Marshall (2000) have also described the spiritual as holistic. They have maintained that the spiritual represents a dynamic wholeness of Self in which Self is at one with itself and with the whole of creation. Further, they have contended that the goal of Western spirituality has been the achievement of this type of unity, or wholeness. They have described the spiritual as being in touch with some whole that is larger and richer, and which puts one's present limited situation into a new perspective. It entails a search for meaning that leads to something more, something beyond that gives meaning to a person's lived experience. Such a holistic concept of the spiritual as representing a dynamic wholeness – of Self at one with Self and the whole of creation – suggests connectedness and relationality not only with Self but also with Other in creation – the universe – and possibly the Transcendent.

The views of the writers referred to above support the notion that spirituality is in fact a natural predisposition of humankind. If this is indeed the case, then it is possible that insights from the process of biological evolution may substantiate this understanding. The following section of this chapter examines this possibility.

A Biological and Evolutional Reality

Studies in the fields of biology, neurological science and evolution support the case that spirituality is a natural human predisposition, arguing that spirituality is present in all people as an attribute that has been selected in the evolution of the human species. It was the British zoologist Alister Hardy who first proposed that what he called religious experience (more commonly termed today as the spiritual, or spiritual experience) has evolved through the process of natural selection because it has survival value for the individual. In other words, the capacity for spirituality is potentially present in all human beings because it has a positive function in enabling human beings to survive in their natural environments, and therefore is an attribute that has been favoured by the process of natural selection. There have been more recent studies which focus on the notions of domain specificity and other neurobiological perspectives which further support Hardy's (1966) thesis.

Domain specificity and expert knowledge bases

In exploring the evolution of the human mind, Hirschfeld and Gelman (1994) have argued that the mind has evolved not as an all-purpose problem solver, but rather as a collection of independent subsystems, or domains, designed to perform specific tasks. They have described a domain as consisting of a body of knowledge that identifies and interprets a categorization of phenomena which are assumed to share certain properties. A domain functions as a stable response to a set of recurring and complex problems faced by an individual. Such a response may involve perceptual, encoding, retrieval, and inferential processes dedicated to that solution.

While there has been some debate as to whether spirituality functions as a means by which individuals can find solutions to problems of meaning and value, thereby rendering it as a form of intelligence (see for example, Emmons 1999, 2000; Fontana 2003; Hyde 2003a, 2004a; Kwilecki 2000; Mayer 2000; Sinetar 2000; Zohar and Marshall 2000), it can be seen from the above description that it is possible such an independent body of knowledge (a domain), specifically relating to the spiritual, has evolved in the composition of the human mind that specifically relates to the spiritual. For instance, Boyer (1994) has argued in favour of a domain that interprets the class of phenomena described as 'religious ideas', which may function as a means by which individuals respond to and solve problems pertaining to religiosity.

Another perspective has come from American psychologist Robert Emmons. While not explicitly employing the term domain specificity, Emmons (1999, 2000) has discussed the notion of spirituality as an 'expert knowledge base'. An expert knowledge base consists of a collection of information within a substantive realm that facilitates the process of adaptation to an environment. According to Emmons, the spiritual consists of at least five such competencies that could conceivably form part of an individual's expert knowledge base. These are: a) the capacity to transcend the physical and material; b) the ability to experience heightened states of consciousness; c) the ability to sanctify everyday experiences; d) the ability to utilize personal spiritual resources to solve problems in living; and e) the capacity to be virtuous. Further, Emmons has cited the existence of spiritually exceptional individuals such as St Teresa of Jesus and Sufi master Ibn Al-'Arabi. Such cases serve as evidence that the spiritual capabilities outlined above can be (and throughout history have been) highly developed in certain individuals.

Neurobiological perspectives

The concept of the evolution of a domain, or expert knowledge base specifically concerned with the spiritual is further supported by recent neurobiological studies that have sought to identify those aspects of the human brain that might be involved in religious or spiritual ideas and perspectives. Persinger (1996) and Ramachandran and Blakeslee (1998) have reported on their research linking heightened activity in the temporal lobes of individuals who have apperceived spiritual experience. They concluded that the temporal lobes might contain neural machinery specifically concerned with religion, or the spiritual. This area of the temporal lobes has been coined by Zohar and Marshall (2000) as the 'God spot' or 'God module'. While the 'God module' may play an essential biological role in spiritual experience, it neither proves nor disproves the existence of God or whether human beings can communicate with a divine source. Also, the research described above is controversial. Fontana (2003) has argued that this type of study would require extensive replication by others before it could be concluded that temporal lobe activity is involved in the experiences reported across cultures and through the centuries that have been labelled as spiritual. Nonetheless, the research of Persinger and of Ramachandran and Blakeslee does suggest that, from a biological perspective, aspects of the human brain may have evolved which render all human beings capable of being spiritual.

More recently, and as the result of extensive research, a slightly different perspective has been offered by the American neurophysiologist Andrew Newberg, and his colleagues Eugene d'Aquili and Victor Rause. They have maintained that the temporal lobes and limbic structures within it are not solely responsible for the complexity and diversity of such spiritual experiences. These researchers have argued that there are potentially many other structures of the brain involved in such experiences. They have identified four association areas of the human brain – the visual, the orientation, the attention, and the verbal conceptual – which interact to produce the mind's spiritual potential. These four association areas are the most complex neurological compositions in the brain. Newberg, d'Aquili and Rause (2001) have argued that all these structures are required in order to explain the vast array of spiritual experiences apperceived by people. For instance, they describe how these structures combine and interact during the state of passive meditation to shield the mind from the intrusion of superfluous sensory input, a process known as 'deafferentation'. In this state, the orientation area lacks the information needed to create the spatial context in which the self can be oriented. Since there would be no line of distinction between the self and the rest of the universe, the mind then perceives a neurological reality consistent with many mystical descriptions of ultimate spiritual union. In such a state, the mind exists without ego in a state of pure undifferentiated awareness.

In discussing the architecture of the brain, Newberg *et al.* (2001) have maintained that the human brain has evolved over millions of years to address issues of survival and adaptation to environment. While acknowledging that the particular structures involved in spiritual experience developed initially from simpler neurological processes that evolved to address more basic survival needs, they nonetheless argue that their potential for spiritual experience always existed. As evolution proceeded, the potential for the spiritual and its usefulness in addressing issues of meaning and value was realized and favoured by the process of natural selection. This supports the original thesis of Alister Hardy maintaining that spirituality has evolved through the process of natural selection because it has a positive function in enabling individuals to survive in their natural environments.

Ultimate Unity

Further, Newberg *et al.* (2001) have described the neurobiology of transcendence as a movement towards Absolute Unitary Being, that is, when Self blends into Other and mind and matter become one and the same. This refers to the states of unity experienced by many of the mystics from various religious traditions of both Eastern and Western cultures. As the result of their exploration of different association areas of the human brain which may become active in producing the mind's spiritual potential, Newberg and his colleagues have proposed the notion of a 'unitary continuum'. At one pole of the continuum, a person may interact with the world and with others, but may experience this interaction as something from which he or she is apart. As that person progresses along the unitary continuum, the sense of separateness becomes less distinct, and could lead to individual experiences of sacredness, and experiences of unity with Other, regardless of whether Other is encountered in community, creation, or in the Transcendent. In the state of Absolute Unitary Being, 'self blends into the other; mind and matter are one and the same' (p.156). Such a notion is consistent with, and describes in neurological terms, the Buddhist state of *anatta* (no-self), or the Christian mystical state of experiencing the presence of God as the ground of one's own being.

Similarly, Austin (2000) explored the possibility of the waking consciousness losing its sense of superficial self, rendering a state of no-self, or complete unity with Other. Consciousness is said to evolve when the superficial self dissolves. When the 'I-Me-Mine' egocentric triad dissolves, novel states of consciousness are said to emerge. Austin referred to two such states – insight-wisdom, or *kensho-satori*, and internal absorption. In such states, all self-centered subjectivities dissolve, leaving the apperception of the world of the other. Released from subjective attachments, the world revealed is one in the form of unburdened clarity. That is, the world as it really is, without self-referent attachments is apperceived, and one can glimpse the reality of things 'as they "really" are' (p.228).

In drawing on such notions as outlined in the research described above, and in exploring the spirituality of young people in a regional setting, de Souza (2004, 2006) has described spirituality as a journey towards Ultimate Unity. Such a movement can be understood to spiral through different layers of connectedness with self, others, the world and possibly with the Transcendent, which generally move forwards towards wider levels, or inwards to deeper levels, but which could recede depending upon the particular contexts of an individual's experiences and responses. de Souza has argued that such forward and inward movement, for some individuals, has the potential to lead to the widest or deepest level of connectedness, where the individual experiences becoming one with Other, that is, Ultimate Unity. These conclusions support particularly the contentions of Andrew Newberg and his colleagues that the neurobiology of transcendence is a movement towards Absolute Unitary Being, when Self blends into Other, and mind and matter become one and the same.

Social evolution (co-evolution)

The biological nature of spirituality and its favoured selection in the process of the evolution of the human species alone may not adequately explain its continual emergence in humankind. Fontana (2003) has argued that the descriptions of spirituality that have been offered by recent psychological and neurobiological scholarship do not necessarily reveal the evolutionary advantage that spirituality might confer upon the human race. He has maintained that such descriptions (particularly in relation to the 'God Spot') seem more concerned with the quality of life than with the physical survival of the human species. Fontana has noted, for instance, that many of the descriptions of spirituality are closely linked with the generation of altruism. Altruism is problematic because it does not necessarily enhance the survival prospects of members of a species, as would be the case with, for example, self-sacrifice. Following this line of thought, Fontana has maintained that if spirituality is linked with altruism, it would be difficult to conceive of it as an attribute that had been selected in the evolution of the human species because it would not necessarily enhance its chances of survival. Yet, scholars such as David Hay and Rebecca Nye have argued that spirituality underlies the altruistic impulse, and that all forms of self-sacrificing behaviour can be viewed as a function of spiritual awareness. There is a need then to examine and take account of additional factors and perspectives, such as the social and cultural component in the evolution of spirituality.

One such perspective can be drawn from the work of anthropologist William Durham who offered a systematic account of the relationship between biological and social evolution, a process known as co-evolution. Durham (1991) asserted that social evolution occurs in a way similar to biological evolution through the process of natural selection. In the case of the former, the units of cultural meaning are known as *memes*. Memes can vary from the most basic units of connotation, through to the more complex ideas, beliefs and value systems. The particular variations of memes within a human group or community – 'allomemes' – provide the different possibilities from which selections can be made in the process of social evolution.

As with genetic variation, not all variations of memes have equal fitness for survival. Durham asserted that whilst natural selection occurs as a type of selection by consequences – organisms that are unfit for survival fail to survive – cultural selection operates as selection according to consequences. Particular patterns of social behaviour are deemed as either helpful or detrimental to survival on the basis of personal experience, history or rational reflection. Social evolution then acts as a guided mechanism of change. It tends to advance human survival and reproduction, and, according to Durham, it does so with significantly greater efficiency than natural selection.

This process of co-evolution may explain in part the continual emergence of spirituality in humankind, particularly as it underlies the altruistic impulse. That is to say, altruism may be a meme that has been selected via the process of social evolution because it has survival value for the human community, and because it has concordance with the underlying biological predisposition to spirituality. However, as Hay and Nye (2006) have noted, in some cases social evolution can have a damaging effect on the survival of a community. Negative social processes can be imposed from influences outside of a community. For example, powerful groups or individuals can coerce others to behave in ways contrary to the mechanism of change promoted by social evolution. There can be occasions on which, in relation to external pressure, there is a voluntary acceptance of memes that are unhelpful to survival. This may create an obstruction, where existing social values that normally promote survival are impeded by factors such as propaganda, advertising, brainwashing, or drug addiction.

It has been the contention of Hay and Nye that spirituality, naturally (biologically) selected in humankind, can be repressed by the socially constructed processes that contradict it in the manner described above. By way of example, they have identified modern individualist philosophy as a meme that has emerged in opposition to biological evolution because of the destructive nature of the societies it has generated. Hay and Nye have suggested that the traditional meme that has constantly been selected for the history of the human species is universalist religion. However, through the processes described above, modern individualist philosophy has emerged and has, in many instances, displaced the naturally selected meme of universalist religion.

Spirituality, social evolution and children

Of relevance to my work is Hay and Nye's (2006) contention that the theory of co-evolution has particular importance in exploring the spirituality of children. Spirituality is a quality selected in the biological evolution of humankind and is therefore a universal human predisposition. Because it is so primal, it is something that can be seen particularly clearly in children. The process of co-evolution in part explains why particular memes – units of cultural meaning – have been selected via the process of social evolution because they have survival value for the human community, and because they have concordance with the underlying biological predisposition to spirituality. This would be the case with a meme such as altruism. However, the process of co-evolution can at times have a detrimental effect on spirituality by selecting memes that work in opposition to the biological predisposition of spirituality. It has been the contention of Hay and Nye, that, in many cases, the spirituality so naturally present in children is being overlaid and repressed by socially constructed processes that contradict it in the manner described above. Social evolution has selected memes that have created a value blockage or displacement to the natural expression of spirituality.

Hay (2001) has further maintained that this suppression of people's spiritual lives has led to the privatization of spirituality. The discarding of spiritual awareness is not a natural phenomenon. It is a social construction of Western culture that needs to be counteracted. Hay has maintained that it is the task of educators in both secular and religious settings to nurture and protect the spiritual dimension of children's lives. The role of the teacher is crucial in reconstructing a climate in which spirituality is nourished.

The Divine at the Core of Self

While much of the contemporary literature has described spirituality in terms of relationality and connectedness, many of the world's mystical and contemplative traditions, both Eastern and Western, have understood spirituality as involving a journey towards unity with Other, or Ultimate Unity (de Souza 2004, 2006), by which, at the deepest levels of connectedness, an individual might experience becoming unified with Other. While an in-depth discussion of these traditions is beyond the scope of this chapter, a few pertinent factors are highlighted below.

Christian mystical tradition

The Christian mystical tradition has for some time understood the unity said to exist between Self and the Divine.[3] For example, in *The Interior Castle,* St Teresa of Jesus (1577) wrote of the soul, the core of Self, as being the place where God dwells, and of prayer as being the means by which the soul is united with God. Similarly, in *Stanzas between the Soul and the Bridegroom (The Whole Canticle)* St John of the Cross (1542–1591) wrote of the soul who has glimpsed the high state of perfection, of union with God. In *The Soul's Journey into God,* St Bonaventure wrote of Jesus Christ as being not only the way of the mystical path, but the one who stands at the ultimate point of the mystical path (Mommaers 2003). Christian mystic Meister Eckhart in his statement succinctly phrased this unity between Self and God, 'The eye with which I see God is the same eye with which God sees me' (Shannon 2003, p.217).

Among the more contemporary mystics of the Christian tradition who have expressed this understanding of Self as being one with the Divine is Thomas Merton. In exploring the quest for self-identity, Merton (1978) wrote of the discovery of the true Self as an experience of finding God. Such a search entailed transcending the superficial self – going beyond the 'I' that represents the ego with its own opinions and ideas, to discover, or recover the 'I' at the depth of one's own being, achieved in Merton's own language as passing through the centre of the soul to find God.

Of particular significance is Merton's concept of ceasing to be conscious of the separateness between Self and God – Other. In seeking to discover, or to rediscover one's true Self, Merton effactually argued that Self becomes unified with the Transcendent Other. In writing of Merton's place of nowhere, Finley (2003) succinctly expressed this concept in stating that 'The true self is rather our whole self before God' (p.23). The more an individual searches for her or his true Self, the more she or he may come to discover that Self and Other are one.

At the centre of each individual's Self, then, is the Divine presence. Therefore, the relationship between Self and others is also pertinent, and renders a significance not just for the Transcendent Other, but also for Other as encountered in both the human and nonhuman world. That is, the Divine at the core of all existence. Again, the writings of Merton express the importance of the relationship between Self and Other. The 'I' that searches to discover God by transcending the superficial self and delving into the deeper core of one's being also discovers the image of the Divine in every other person and in the whole of creation. By journeying into the depths of one's being to discover God, humankind may come to discover who others really are.

Shannon (2003) describes Merton's understanding this as the ultimate unity of all reality. The world, although distinct from God, is not separate from God. People, although individual and unique, are not separate from God because God is the source and ground of humankind's being. Therefore, 'Because we are one with God, we are also one with one another...you are one with God. I am one with God. It follows that we are one with one another' (p.217).

Another contemporary Christian mystic who has expressed this understanding of Self as being one with the Divine is Bede Griffiths. In exploring the Hindu-Christian dialogue, Griffiths (1984) maintained that the search for God entails a continual effort to discover the reality of the hidden presence of God in the depths of the soul. It is there that one must 'make the discovery of Christ as the Atman, the true Self, of every being' (p.24). For Griffiths, Christ is at the centre of Self, and provides a point of meeting not just for the individual and God, but the individual and other people, as well as the whole of creation. For in Christ a person discovers not only the centre or ground of his or her own being, but also a meeting point with all people and with the whole world of nature. That is to say, Griffiths has affirmed the presence of the Divine in Other and, therefore, spirituality may become an expression of connectedness with Other. According to Griffiths, the means by which the individual attains, or realizes this unity with the Divine at the centre of Self is through prayer and contemplation.

Eastern traditions

Eastern philosophy has long understood the spiritual path to involve Self and its true nature. In Buddhism, significant emphasis is placed upon the individual being able to see through the illusory, conditioned self so as to realize one's true nature. Once a person recognizes the illusory nature of her or his relative and socially constructed self, there comes an awareness that in its place exists an expansive state of being. Such a state of being is understood to be an integral part of the unified whole which is ultimate reality. One is said to arrive at this state through intensive meditative practices. The Buddhist term for this state is *anatta*, meaning no-self (Hill, Knitter and Madges 2002). This means that the self ceases to exist as a distinct and separate entity. Self blends into Other, and mind and matter become one and the same. This state is understood to be one's true nature, and in becoming aware of it, a person might become aware of the true nature of everything else.

Hindus traditionally refer to 'self' in lower case letters, signifying the conditioned and socially constructed self that results from a person's learned experiences and reactions to those experiences. It is the 'self' that a person mistakenly takes to be who he or she really is. It refers to the ego which seeks to make itself 'master of the world' (Griffiths 2002, p.16). In speaking of 'Self' with an initial capital, Hindus refer to a person's own true nature which is understood to be identified with the Absolute, the Brahman (Billington 1997). It is the indwelling Self, the Divine light, mysteriously present and shining in each person (Zohar and Marshall 2000). Self is understood to be one with the Brahman. Hart (2003) has drawn attention to the Hindu tenet, Atman and Brahman are one, meaning that the individual human and the Godhead are one and the same. From this, Hart has concluded that the spiritual path 'involves realizing more of this innate divinity as we uncoil the multidimensional nature of ourselves and the universe' (p.114). Griffiths

(2002) has maintained that the unity of the Atman and the Brahman is a key feature of Indian thought. Self – the Atman – the Ground of personal being is one with the Brahman, the Ground of universal being. In further exploring the concept of the Divine as being one with Self, de Souza (2005) has maintained that the above understanding is reflected in the Indian greeting, *Namaste*, which in loose translation may be rendered as 'The Divine Presence in me meets the Divine Presence in you. I bow to the Divine Presence in you' (p.42).

The insights from Eastern traditions allude to the individual being able to expand her or his awareness so as to transcend or move beyond the superficial self – the ego – in order to realize the true Self, or in Merton's language, to pass through the centre of the soul in order to find God. Literature from the biological perspectives has explained in neurological terms those parts of the human brain that might become active when this occurs. Such an activity involves the notion of consciousness, and the possibility of attaining higher levels of consciousness in order to realize the true Self. While acknowledging the complexity and uncertainty associated in a discussion of the nature of consciousness and Self, the following perspectives drawn from Eastern philosophy, integrated in some instances with Western science, are presented as they have relevance for my understanding of spirituality.

Eastern philosophical perspectives on consciousness

Several writers have indicated the Eastern notion of different, and sometimes interconnected, levels of consciousness that might be attained by the individual in order to realize the true or centre of Self. For example, the Eastern philosopher Sri Aurobindo has drawn attention to notion of ascending planes of consciousness from *matter* to *satchitananda*. These planes include the material plane, the vital plane, the mental plane, the transitional planes of higher mind, the illuminated mind, the intuitive mind and Overmind, the Supramental plane, and the divine consciousness.[4] According to Aurobindo, each human being is a self-developing soul, evolving towards greater divinity (Marshak and Litfin 2002). It is when a person reaches the level of divine consciousness that he or she might be said to have arrived at the highest status of his or her real, or true Self.

Similarly, Fontana (2003) has noted that a feature among the major Eastern traditions and Western esoteric traditions is the notion of developmental levels of consciousness, most clearly outlined in the Advaita Vendanta school of Hinduism. This particular model of consciousness has six major levels, each, with the exception of the last, containing several subdivisions. At the lowest point is the material level, at which consciousness is identified solely with the sensory. This is followed by the vital level, at which consciousness becomes aware of itself. At the discriminatory level, consciousness begins to categories objects and events presented by experience. It is also at this level that consciousness distinguishes between turning inward towards the nonmaterial realm of thought, intuition, and perhaps spiritual awareness, and outward toward the material world. At the ratiocinative level consciousness acquires the capacity for analytical and rational thought. The causal level entails consciousness experiencing pure contentless awareness, or consciousness in and of itself. At the highest level – the Brahmanic level – consciousness is said to be aware of reality as a unified field of energy in which the material, the individual, and the Absolute, or Brahman, are in essence identical with each other.

Wilber's Integral Theory of Consciousness

In discussing the different waves, lines and states that might comprise an integral theory of consciousness, transpersonal psychologist Ken Wilber has made a sustained and authentic attempt to link the notion of developmental levels of consciousness that are recognized in the East, for example those outlined in the Advaita Vedanta model, with Western science. Rather than envisaging these levels of consciousness as hierarchical, Wilber has described these developmental levels as a holarchy from matter to life to mind to soul to spirit, arranged along what he terms the 'great rainbow or spectrum' (Wilber 2000a, p.148) of consciousness. Along this spectrum, Wilber has incorporated key aspects of many of the major psychological and wisdom traditions – Eastern and Western, as well as ancient and modern. Across this spectrum, the higher levels of consciousness are understood to enfold the preceding levels.[5] Wilber has maintained that this type of thinking reflects the work of Aurobindo, who had argued that spiritual evolution conformed to a logic of successive unfolding. The higher, transpersonal levels of consciousness do not sit on top of lower levels, but rather, as these higher levels of consciousness unfold, they envelop the lower levels. These levels, or 'waves' as Wilber has described them, have been termed developmental not because they are rigid, linear, or appear as rungs-in-the-ladder, but rather because they are fluid, and overlap as waves appear to do. These developmental levels or waves therefore appear to be like 'concentric spheres of increasing embrace, inclusion, and holistic capacity' (p.147).

Central to this notion of developmental waves of consciousness is Wilber's notion of Self, or self-system, which acts as a means by which to integrate, or balance these waves of consciousness. Wilber has maintained that levels or waves of consciousness, as well as other aspects of awareness, appear to be devoid of an intrinsic self-sense. One of the primary characteristics of Self is its capacity to identify with the basic levels, or waves of consciousness. This drive to integrate the various components of the psyche is a fundamental feature of the self-system. Wilber has envisaged Self as a centre of gravity, with the various levels, lines and states of consciousness orbiting around the integrating tendency of Self. He has also argued that Self also undergoes its own type of development through what might be considered as a series of waves. However, the distinguishing feature of Self is its ability to coordinate all of this into a coherent whole.

An understanding of an integral theory of consciousness enhances the credibility of the existence of different levels, or waves of consciousness. It serves to broaden the perspective and include levels other than the three that have been widely referred to in Western psychological literature: conscious, subconscious, and unconscious. Wilber has further suggested that this integral theory of consciousness, with its notion of Self and the integrating tendency of Self, has the potential to assist in explaining how Self, through integrating higher levels of consciousness with lower levels, might achieve unity with the Absolute, the true Self. That is to say, Self becomes one with Other, where in the Buddhist tradition, one attains the state of *anatta*, or no self, or where in the Hindu understanding, Atman and Brahman become one, or where in Christian mystical terms, one passes through the centre of soul in order to find God.

While many scholars have put forward the notion that spirituality is concerned with a sense of connectedness and relationality with Self, others, the world, and possibly with the Transcendent, my understanding, informed by the literature detailed above, is that spirituality is concerned with more than connectedness. Spirituality is concerned with that movement towards Ultimate Unity (de Souza 2004, 2006), whereby at the deepest and widest levels of connectedness, an individual may experience unity with Other. The notion of connectedness, or relationality, implies two objects being in relationship or connected to each other. Ultimate Unity, however, implies one – becoming one with Other.[6] The means by which Ultimate Unity may be attained involves the successive unfolding of higher levels of consciousness, which may enable the individual to transcend the ego in order to realize the true Self which is unified with Other.

In a Nutshell

Through this chapter I have explored an understanding of spirituality from three broad perspectives – the relationship between spirituality and institutional Christianity, spirituality as a natural human predisposition, and the Divine at the core of Self. In the light of this, I would like to offer three particular descriptions of spirituality which reflect my understanding of this term – that spirituality is an essential human trait, that it concerns the movement towards Ultimate Unity, and that spirituality is given outward expression.

1. Spirituality is an essential human trait

Spirituality is an ontological and biological reality. It is a natural human predisposition involving a path towards the realization of one's true Self in which ultimately Self is unified with everything that is Other than Self. It involves the successive unfolding of higher levels of consciousness which, at the highest levels, may enable the individual to transcend the ego in order to apperceive the deepest and widest levels of connectedness in which Self and Other are unified. The continual emergence of spirituality in humankind may in part also be explained by the process of co-evolution. Behaviours and attributes which have concordance with the underlying biological predisposition to spirituality have continued to be selected as they have a positive value in enabling individuals to survive in their environments.

2. Spirituality concerns the movement towards Ultimate Unity

Spirituality is understood to involve more than connectedness and relationality. It is concerned with that movement towards Ultimate Unity, whereby at the deepest and widest levels of connectedness, an individual may experience unity with Other. As noted, the notion of connectedness, or relationality, implies two objects being in relationship or connected to each other. Ultimate Unity, however, implies one. It entails the individual becoming one with Other. The means by which Ultimate Unity may be attained involves the successive unfolding of higher levels of consciousness, which may enable the individual to transcend the ego in order to realize the true Self which is unified with Other.

The notion of Ultimate Unity has been argued in this chapter on a number of grounds. In a religious sense, practitioners of both Eastern and Christian traditions have sought and described this type of unity with Other, in which, at the deepest and widest levels of connectedness, Self becomes one with Other. However, as also noted in this chapter, some literature suggests that individuals who are not declared adherents of any particular faith tradition are capable of apperceiving experiences along the unitary continuum since the capacity for an individual to do so has evolved biologically, and involves the neurological function of various sites within the human brain.

3. Spirituality is given expression

Spirituality is also understood to be the outward expression of this sense of unity, possibly, although not necessarily, through a formal system of values and beliefs, that is, institutional religion. Spirituality is the outward expression of the fire within the soul in terms of how one might act in relation to the human and nonhuman world, and towards a Transcendent dimension. Typically, such expression might be characterized by altruism and acts of selflessness.

The above descriptions indicate how spirituality is to be understood within this book. My understanding is that children's spirituality is an ontological reality and involves a path towards the realization of the true Self, in which ultimately, Self is unified with everything that is Other than Self. This unity can be expressed both outwardly and inwardly in terms of different levels of connectedness towards Other, and in some instances, this expression could reflect the deepest levels of connectedness, whereby the individual may experience becoming one with Other, that is, Ultimate Unity.

Following such a line of thought, I use 'Self' with an initial upper case letter to refer to the individual's true nature, which, at the deepest level, can be understood to be one with the Divine, or God in the Christian tradition. I utilize 'self' with an initial lower letter case to refer to the socially constructed self, the ego, or persona out of which a person might commonly act. Since the Divine, or Absolute, can be understood to be one with each other person's Self, I use 'Other' with an initial upper case letter in referring to Other in both the human and nonhuman, with whom Self seeks to become unified.[7]

CHAPTER 3

Research on the Spirituality of Childhood

There is a growing body of research which contributes to what is already known about the spirituality of children. In recent times Western secularized countries in particular have shown an interest in learning more about the spiritual dimension of childhood. The reasons for this are many and varied. In England and Wales the need to investigate children's spirituality arose largely in relation to educational legislation, particularly the 1998 Education Reform Act, which issued a mandate that all schools must have balanced and broadly based curricula promoting the spiritual, moral, cultural, mental and physical development of students. In the United States of America, concern for the moral direction of young people has been a pressing issue, especially in light of events such as the Columbine massacre in which two teenage students randomly opened fire upon their fellow classmates, before ending their own lives. This event, and others like it, led to a recognition that for many, life lacked a sense of meaning and purpose and that a spiritual dimension of life needs to be rekindled and nurtured. In countries like Australia and New Zealand, questions concerning the spiritual well being of children and adolescents have begun to arise in relation to the coping mechanisms of youth, where it has been argued that a sense of connectedness with family and community can act as a protective factor and a means by which to build resilience in the young.[8]

In this chapter I present and discuss some of this research that has explored the spirituality of children and young people. My aim is not to explore the entire range of empirical study, but rather to show how some of these various investigations have, in different ways, specifically influenced my own research, as well as to provide a field of inquiry in which to situate my own study.

Religious Language and Concepts

All researchers are products of the contexts in which they find themselves conducting their investigations. Since the connection between spirituality and religion has traditionally been considered close, as discussed in the previous chapter, much of the early research into children's spirituality tended to assume that expressions of spirituality were dependent upon the use of religious language and concepts. That is to say, researchers tended to look for evidence of spirituality in the language and concepts which pertained to religion and which were drawn upon by the participants. The following examples of research studies are indicative of this type of understanding.

The work of David Heller

American psychologist David Heller conducted a study during the latter half of the 1980s, investigating children's conceptions of God. Assuming the role of an observer-participant, Heller (1986) conducted semi-structured interviews with 40 children (20 boys and 20 girls) of four different religious backgrounds – Catholic, Jewish, Protestant (Baptist) and Hindu (American Ashram Group). Heller met with each of these children once in a two-hour interview. The interview itself consisted of six segments, each of which was designed to collect particular data related to aspects of these children's religious imagery: naming the deity, drawing the deity, storytelling about the deity, playing the deity, questions and answers about the deity, and letters to the deity. While Heller's personal perspective was openly religious, he took care to ensure that the children used their own terms and language, and that they related them to other issues of personal significance.

Through the interviews with the 40 children who took part in this study, Heller discovered a rich array of spiritual imagery. Many of the children conversed quite spontaneously about God and about matters that offered insight into their personal search for meaning. For example, in responding to a query regarding the death of an older person, an 11-year-old girl openly noted 'God takes away people's suffering, like from cancer. He has the power to do that and he uses death in that way. But he must not have full control – otherwise he would cure the cancer' (p.108).

Similarly, Heller noted that, in discussing 'light' as a recurring theme which emerged from the interviews, one nine-year-old child described light as being warm and that it enabled him to feel good about himself. This participant described light as being within himself, and that it could shine even when tragedy would strike, '...like when my sister died, it still can shine. I can't say I feel this all the time – but when I feel it I feel it very strong [look of enchantment]' (p.128).

The investigation of Robert Coles

Among others who have attempted to provide insight into the spiritual lives of children is American child psychiatrist Robert Coles. In his large-scale study, Coles (1990) engaged in numerous conversations with children between the ages of 6 and 13 from a variety of countries, including the United States of America, South America, Europe, the Middle East and Africa. The children came from a variety of cultural and religious backgrounds, including Christian, Islamic and Jewish. Coles described his work as an investigation of the different ways in which children process spiritual matters. The emphasis was not so much on children as students or practitioners of a particular religious tradition, but on children as being soulful in the ways they reveal themselves as spiritual beings. In dialogue with children, Coles placed his emphasis on listening attentively to the descriptions of these children's experiences and on their understandings of what they meant when they spoke of God. He therefore allowed the children to articulate for themselves their ultimate concerns. In many cases the children's religious customs and beliefs came up in discussion. However, for many of the children, an interest in God, the supernatural, the ultimate meaning of life as well as an interest in the sacred was not necessarily mediated by religious practice. Some of the children belonged to what might be described as typically 'religious' families, although Coles noted that at times they asked questions that were not necessarily in keeping with the tenets of their religion. Some children were the sons or daughters of parents who were professed atheists or agnostics, yet nonetheless indicated an interest and curiosity about God and the sacred.

As a result of his conversations with these many children from such an array of cultural and religious backgrounds, Coles came to view spiritual awareness as a universal human predisposition. The children with whom he spoke expressed in their own way their understanding and indeed concern about spiritual matters. For example, after a lengthy period of two years, a Hopi Indian girl expressed to Coles her understanding of spirituality as a connectedness between her people, the land and her notion of God – 'Our God is the sky, and lives wherever the sky is. Our God is the sun and the moon too, and our God is our people, if we remember to stay here on the land' (p.25).

Coles understood it to be a mistake to give first place to cognition, that is, to intellectual operations in attempting to understand children's spirituality. Rather, he maintained the importance of actively listening to the children themselves, and of resisting the urge to overlay one's own interpretation on the experiences these children described.

The work of Coles has presented something of the landscape of the spiritual lives of children. While he hesitated to generalize and draw conclusions, Coles articulated his belief in religious language as providing a framework for discussing spiritual matters, and as being one possible expression of a child's spirituality. He maintained there to be an overlap for many children between their religious life and their spiritual life, and argued this to be the case even when children appeared to have no typically religious affiliation whatsoever.

The above examples of research have assumed, either implicitly or explicitly, that spirituality is expressed largely through the use of religious language and concepts. This in part has been due to the language the researchers themselves have used in designing and communicating their projects. Spirituality has been understood and identified as an expression of religion by many investigators. Hence, much of the research on children's spirituality, until more recent times, has focused on 'God talk'. However, if spirituality is a natural human predisposition concerned with the relational dimension of being, and is given expression outwardly, then it is an attribute present in all people regardless of their religious affiliation and belief or non-belief in a higher power. In other words, spirituality can be expressed outside of a mainstream religious tradition. Such an understanding is important given the secular nature of countries like Great Britain, the United States of America, Australia, New Zealand, and Canada in which research into the field of children's spirituality has been conducted.

In taking this into account, some of the more recent research into the spirituality of children has taken a different direction. Such investigations have focused not so much on the expression of religious language and concepts as indicators of spirituality. Rather, these studies have focused on the perceptions, awareness and responses of children to what might be classified as ordinary and everyday activities in looking for clues to the spiritual domain in the lives of children.

Perceptions, Awareness and Responses to Everyday Phenomena

The following examples of research, which I present and discuss below, are indicative of investigations which have focused on the perceptions, awareness and responses of children to ordinary, everyday phenomena in exploring their spirituality.

Talking to children about things spiritual

Beginning with a description of spirituality as an awareness of something other, something greater than the course of everyday events, British researcher Elaine McCreery entered into conversation with young schoolchildren, aged between four and five, about the world as they understood it (1996). She selected a range of familiar experiences for discussion, as well as activities for engagement in which spiritual aspects might arise. Such experiences included events in the home (birth, death, love, trust), at school (stories, nature study, companionship) and on television (cultural difference, violence, noble behaviour, and the like). These experiences, along with activities such as painting, drawing, sorting, matching, singing, storytelling, and so forth, were included in each of a number of sessions with small groups of children. It was hoped that the children's participation in these sessions might enable the identification of some ways of entering into young children's conception of the spiritual.

Importantly, in her conversations with children, McCreery was careful to allow them to use their own words, thereby avoiding language that might influence their responses. McCreery was especially careful to avoid the use of religious language – 'God talk' – in these conversations. She was interested in learning the words and phrases the children themselves used to express their spiritual knowing. If the children used religious language themselves, then McCreery would explore it with them, but would not furnish them with it. For example, in talking about death with the children, McCreery considered a question such as, 'What do you think happens when we die?' as being too leading. A question of this nature could have introduced to the children the religious connotations of death. Instead, McCreery felt it better to tell a story, involving a little girl and the death of her pet cat. The children were then invited to offer a reflection on this by responding to the question: 'Julie was very upset after her cat was killed; what could we say to make her feel better?' (p.201).

In this particular example, McCreery found that the children related the story of the little girl and the death of her cat to their own lives. They spoke freely about the death of their own pets, grandparents, and in one instance, the death of a baby sister. The children expressed an understanding of the notion that once dead, a person, or animal, cannot return to life. They also related some knowledge about the dead going to the sky to be with Jesus and God.

One particular notion that seemed to occur frequently in the discussion on death was the connection of death with the hospital.

While acknowledging that further investigation was necessary, McCreery noted that the use of stories relating to the children's own life experience was an effective strategy to use in this type of research. In using such a technique, McCreery found that, even at very young ages, children have begun to sort their experiences of the world, and they have begun to ask questions about those aspects they do not yet understand. From this investigation, McCreery pointed out that the development of the spiritual lives of these young children needs to begin with the questions they themselves ask as they begin their encounter with the world. Those who work and engage with children must then find ways of encouraging such questions. They must also determine ways of exploring these types of questions and issues with children when and as they arise. In this way, McCreery argued, we can be sure we are addressing the spiritual dimension of children's lives in ways that are meaningful for them.

The Children and Worldviews Project

As researchers involved in the *Children and Worldviews Project*, Clive and Jane Erricker and their colleagues have contended that the ways in which children learn are inseparable from who they are and the experiences that have shaped their identity. Focusing on education, they have argued that if teachers wish to plan a curriculum that takes as its starting point where the children are 'at', they need to take into account more than the existing knowledge of the learners. Educators need also to consider the interpretive frameworks of the learners. Such frameworks, they have argued, include the ways in which children attempt to understand and make sense of important existential issues. If existential issues form a part of such a framework, the Errickers and their colleagues have suggested that one might be said to be considering aspects of children's spirituality.

The Children and Worldviews Project team maintained that truth, for children, was related to their personal narratives that had been constructed out of their individual experience. They argued that children already possess a narrative within which they construct meaning, and that it is therefore meaning in preference to truth or knowledge that underpins a holistic education. In their view, educators then cannot impose a narrative upon children which does not engage with the children's own narrative. Neither can they insist upon a rationality which does not make sense in terms of the way the children have constructed meaning from their experiences (Erricker *et al.* 1997). This is not to undermine the importance of instruction or enculturation. These are pertinent, but cannot be addressed independently of an engagement with the evolving worldviews of children.

In their qualitative research, Erricker and Erricker (1996) utilized unstructured interviews with small groups of children. They were eager that these children should be allowed to speak in as natural and unstructured way as possible. The data generated would then enable them to construct theory (a grounded theory approach). After examining the data provided by the children's conversations focusing on the existential themes of loss and conflict, they identified a set of 'genres' that these children tended to utilize, and within which their spirituality must find expression. For example, one of the genres tentatively assigned to the children interviewed was the notion of the all-American kid, whose life tended to revolve around theme parks, Macdonald's fast food and other aspects of consumerism. In contrast, another of the genres identified was the family-centred genre, in which relationships within the family were considered to be of primary importance.

While not suggesting that children always operate only in one particular genre, the Errickers and their colleagues have maintained that the identification of such genres helps in gaining insight into a child's approach to life. They have stressed the importance of listening and speaking to children in coming to an understanding of their spirituality and the ways in which educators might nurture this in the classroom context. They have maintained their research has convinced them that, should the thinking of children not be taken seriously in relation to their particular experiences and ideas, teachers do them and education a disservice.

The work of David Hay and Rebecca Nye

One major investigation, which has sought this type of new direction, is that of David Hay and Rebecca Nye, two researchers from Britain, who reported on a three-year children's spirituality project at the University of Nottingham. In using a grounded theory approach, the intention of their investigation was to develop a theoretical interpretation of children's spirituality, based on the reflections of what the children themselves who took part in this study said in conversation with the field worker, Rebecca Nye. In particular, this research was in response to the 1998 Education Reform Act, England and Wales, which issued a mandate that schools must have balanced and broadly based curricula promoting the spiritual, moral, cultural, mental and physical development of students.

The researchers were interested in conversing with children representative of the range of religious and secular perspectives likely to be found in state schools in Britain. In total, they held conversations with 38 children: nine boys and nine girls between the ages of six and seven, and ten boys and ten girls between the ages of ten and eleven. Approximately three quarters of these children were classified as having no religious affiliation, four were classified as Church of England, four were Muslim and two Roman Catholic.

In undertaking this research, Hay and Nye (2006) expressed their acute awareness of the fact that in Western culture, the world into which children are socialized is often destructive of their spirituality, as has been discussed in the previous chapter. These researchers also expressed their awareness of the fact that children growing up in today's Western world may be unlikely to use traditional religious language and discourse to express elements of their spiritual life.

To begin, then, Hay and Nye proposed three interrelated themes or categories of spiritual sensitivity as a 'sketch map' of those areas of human experience that may act as media for spirituality. These categories provided a starting point in terms of what to look for in their conversations with children, have been influenced by the work of Donaldson (1992) and were developed further from these researchers' earlier work (Nye and Hay 1996). The first of these categories was 'awareness sensing', which involves attending to the here and now of experience. It includes alertness to what might be experienced in moments of concentration or stillness. The second was 'mystery sensing', pertaining to the wonder and awe, the fascination and questioning which is characteristic of children as they interact with the mystery of the universe. It also pertains to the use of imagination – one means by which children may transcend, or go beyond, their everyday experiences. The third area was 'value sensing', referring to the moral sensitivity of children. It encompasses the delight and despair that express children's sense of goodness or evil. Value sensing also includes a sense of that which really matters to the children themselves – that which is of ultimate meaning and value to them in their lives.

As a result of their research investigating the spirituality of children, Hay and Nye noted and described surprisingly high levels of consciousness or perceptiveness exhibited in their conversations. These conversations were embedded in the context of how the child connected or related to themselves, to other people, to the world and to the Transcendent (God). They coined the term 'relational consciousness' to describe this quality of the children's spirituality.

Two particular characteristics of these children's relational consciousness were commented upon. The first was the individuality of each child's spirituality. It was possible to identify for each child a personal 'signature' that pertained to that child's spirituality. This was referred to in the study as the 'signature phenomenon'. This led to the conclusion that each of the children in the study presented different expressions of spirituality, each active in its own way. Hay and Nye concluded that one then needs to attend to each child's personal style if one is to experience their spirituality. In other words, the spirituality of a child is uniquely dependent upon the contours of his or her personal psychology. This links with the research of the Errickers and their colleagues (1997), and their emphasis on the need to listen carefully to children in order to understand their spirituality.

The second feature of these children's relational consciousness discussed by Hay and Nye was their ability and readiness to draw on religious language and ideas in making meaning of their discussed experiences. This feature emerged, even though many of the children had little or no background knowledge and experience of formal religion. Hay and Nye noted that their use of religious dialogue could include the explicit use of religious language and terminology, or it could include what they describe as implicit spiritual discourse. The latter involved conversation where, although the dialogue may have lacked clear traditional religious or metaphysical terminology, the child was able to express sensitive, profound and philosophical reflections concerning ultimate meaning and value.

Listening to...listening for...

Canadian scholar Elaine Champagne has investigated the spiritual dimension of the lives of very young children in a secular setting, using as a starting point some ordinary and everyday observed experiences of children. Champagne (2001) has argued that while it is possible to listen to the expressions of spirituality the children themselves reveal in conversation, it is also possible to listen *for* the spiritual underlying their everyday lives. In reflecting upon the observations of children, she has presented three characteristic dimensions of spirituality that might be encountered in such a listening to and for: spirituality as human experience, spirituality as a quest for unification and integrity, and spirituality as a quality of consciousness.

Champagne has pointed out that spiritual experience is human experience, and that spirituality cannot be dissociated from human experience. Yet, at the same time, spirituality points to that which is beyond the human. In other words, spirituality is both immanent and transcendent.

Spirituality is also a search for unification and integrity. Champagne has noted that an individual's spirituality has the potential to muster inner resources towards a more unified and harmonious existence. Spirituality can then act as a basis for growth towards becoming a relational human being, pointing to what a person may consider as the ultimate value. In the Christian context, this search for unification and integrity enables a person not only to relate to themselves and others, but also to the Ultimate Other, God.

Spirituality as a quality of consciousness refers to the capacity of a person to reflect, to maintain a distance from, or describe an experience, and the capacity of abstraction. Champagne has noted that while most cognitive theories suggest that these capacities have generally not yet developed in young children, there is a sense in which young children can and do display such capabilities, even before they have acquired the formal language to express them. Champagne has drawn on Hay and Nye's (2006) categories of spiritual sensitivity as experiential categories that point to such capabilities in young children. As with Hay and Nye, Champagne has noted that children appear to have relational and conscious intuitions at an early age. Very young children seem to be aware of, and have an implicit understanding of their relationship to their environment long before they are able to name it.

Champagne has noted that these characteristics, or dimensions, were identifiable in each of the children she observed. For example, the experiences of the children observed belonged to the human realm. They were, at a cursory glance, ordinary and everyday experiences. Yet at the same time, each of these children's experiences transcended the human, pointing to something beyond. The children's search for unification and integrity was evident in their openness and eagerness to discover and engage in their world. This pointed to the richer and more complex reality to which they were relating. Spirituality as a quality of consciousness was identifiable in each child's relational way of being – their sense of connection to others and to their world.

Several important issues regarding young children and spirituality can be raised as a result of this research. Chief among them is the question of how one might recognize and give witness to the spiritual dimension of what children express, particularly when their verbal language is limited and often needs to be translated. In acknowledging that further work needs to be undertaken, Champagne maintained that one fundamental question that needs to be asked is whether adults are willing to consider young children as being capable of making sense of their lives, and capable of a creative way of addressing life independently of what adults may have taught them.

More recently, Champagne (2003) has expanded upon her initial research by suggesting, from a phenomenological and hermeneutic approach, that children's spirituality is rooted in the concept of *being*. Analysis of the data of her research has highlighted three spiritual modes of the child's being – Sensitive, Relational and Existential.

The Sensitive mode refers to the way in which young children perceive their environment and the way in which they express themselves while living in those surroundings. It includes the perceptions and expressions of children through their different senses. Parents, care-givers, siblings and peers constitute a significant part of the surroundings of young children with which they interact. The Relational mode of being addresses the quality of such interactions from a spiritual perspective. The Existential mode of being refers to the experiencing of life in time and space. As sensitive and relational beings, young children are active participants in their own existence, for example, through games.

Champagne has argued that the Sensitive, Relational and Existential modes of being have the capability of rendering significant adults in the lives of children – parents, educators and others who engage with children – effective witnesses of their spirituality. Further, Champagne has agued that nurturing the spiritual lives of young children by being attentive to these modes of being may in turn enhance the spiritual awareness of those who care for them.

The secret spiritual world of children

In a large scale research project, American psychologist Tobin Hart collected in-depth interviews from children, as well as written accounts from adults recollecting childhood experiences, that detailed spiritual moments and experiences of those individuals. Rejecting the assumptions of many psychologists that children cannot have spiritual lives prior to the development of formal reasoning, this research suggested that children do in fact possess rich and formative spiritual lives.

Through his research, Hart (2003) identified five spiritual capacities through which children's spirituality seemed to naturally flow: wisdom, wonder/awe, the relationship between one's Self and the Other, seeing the invisible, and wondering in relation to the ultimate questions of life.

Wisdom referred to that way of knowing that emerges through an opening of heart and mind. While it is often assumed that wisdom derives from years of life experience, Hart maintained that wisdom refers also to the child's capacity for being able to get to the heart of the matter. Although children may not have the language or thinking capacity of adults, they seem to possess the capacity to be open to the deep currents of consciousness.

Wonder refers to the way in which the world is sensed by children and involves an array of feelings such as awe, connection, and insight as well as a deep sense of joy. While they can be difficult to describe, Hart has argued that experiences of wonder act as a cornerstone for a spiritual life. Further, Hart has maintained that during such experiences the boundaries can blur between Self and everything Other than Self. Hart recounted one child's description of standing in the water at the beach, moving back and forth with the motion of the waves. When her father had asked what it was she was doing, she had stated simply that she *was* the water. She was unable to explain it in any other way. Such a description accords with the notion of spirituality as a movement towards Ultimate Unity (de Souza 2004, 2006), discussed in Chapter 2 of this book. This child had experienced becoming one with Other. From this, Hart has concluded that although the spiritual has often been portrayed as separate from the world, the wonderings and experiences of this child indicate that the 'other' world is embedded in the here and now.

The relationship between Self and Other, or in Hart's language, 'between you and me' refers to the relational understanding of spirituality in which the spiritual life is lived out at the intersection between one's own life and that of Other. This relational understanding entails how one treats Other and how people treat one another. It is about the sense of compassion and empathy one has for Other. Despite some developmental theorists insisting that children tend to be self-centred and are incapable of empathy and compassion, Hart has argued that young children do have a capacity to feel care and concern for Other, whether Other is to be found in another human being, or in an aspect of nature.

Hart's notion of wondering entails a consideration of questions of ultimate concern, of ultimate meaning and value. Such questions could include 'Why am I here?' or 'What happens when I die?' Children are natural philosophers who frequently wonder about the larger existential questions of life. For many people, the spiritual quest is focused and explored through the wonderings in relation to such questions. While acknowledging that psychologists like Piaget would maintain that children lack the ability to reason and reflect with any degree of sophistication, Hart maintained that such an understanding is incomplete. While they may not possess the adult logic and language, Hart argued that his research indicates children show a capacity for thoughtful consideration of existential questions of meaning and value, and that they are able to comprehend at a deep level.

Hart contended that the universe is multidimensional and mysterious, beyond the ability of humans to measure or imagine. Seeing the invisible refers to the awareness of some children to experience some of these different dimensions. Hart's use of the term indicates that in some way, children are able to tune in to the more subtle levels of reality as they see visions, feel energy, know things at a distance, and find insightful inspiration. Among the many instances cited by Hart to demonstrate this spiritual capacity, is the experience of Laura, a three-year-old child who sees lights and colours around people. Further, Laura's mother insisted that Laura was then able to interpret these colours, indicating what they meant about each person.

However, Hart also issued a cautionary note in relation to seeing the invisible. He has warned of the possibility of becoming overly fascinated by such capabilities, maintaining that those who fixate on developing such psychic abilities without simultaneously developing compassion, intellect and emotional maturity may become preoccupied with their own achievement, a feature that can ultimately be destructive of one's spiritual life. Developing one's spiritual potential means integrating and balancing the different aspects of one's Self. The focus of spirituality needs to be on the ordinary and everyday facets of life that might enable a person to relate to others. Capabilities like seeing the invisible can be detrimental unless they are balanced by compassion, empathy and the like, and enable the individual to better relate to Self and everything that is Other than Self.

Retrospective spiritual narratives

In a similar vein to the above research, Canadian scholar Daniel Scott researched the spiritual dimension of young people's lives by collecting recalled childhood spiritual experiences as a means by which to explore the qualities and characteristics of the spirituality of the young. While the narratives collected by Scott (2004), 22 in total, were from adults, many of them describe incidences from childhood. As with the work of Robinson (1977) and Hart (2003), Scott found that these narratives touched on a range of experiences, including death, mortality, visions, as well as perceptions and connections beyond Self.

Some of the storytellers in Scott's investigation drew explicitly upon religious language in recounting their experience. For example, Ben (six at the time of the experience) described suffering through a severe childhood infection, and turned to God for help. Other participants in Scott's research drew upon the language available in their culture in describing their spiritual experience. For example, Merle (ten at the time of the experience) was winded in a fall from a wall, and heard an inner voice chanting over and over 'Who am I?'

In presenting these experiences, Scott noted that in many instances, they were life-shaping for the individual. For example, Joyce (three at the time of the experience) described how the wonder of the full moon in the middle of the night has remained with her throughout her life. This accords with the work of James (1977), who argued that the spiritual experiences apperceived by the individual often remained vivid memories for the whole of the person's life. Nonetheless, Joyce, like many of the other participants in Scott's study, chose to keep her spiritual life private, maintaining that speaking of spiritual matters prompted others, particularly her parents, to persuade her to discard her inner life. The question of how adults respond to children's spiritual experience is viewed by Scott as crucial in terms of how the adult response can shape the lives of the children themselves, and consequently, their confidence in their consciousness and perception. He maintained that children commonly have significant responses to the ordinary events of life, many of which could potentially be spiritual. Children who apperceive spiritual experience need adults who can demonstrate the capacity to listen, and to take them seriously. One of Scott's participants, Rita (ten at the time of her experiences), commonly experienced premonitions in dreams. However, rather than offering support and guidance, her grandmother acted so as to construct a ring of silence around these dreams, effactually repressing this aspect of Rita's spirituality. As a result, Rita no longer spoke to anyone about her dreams. As she continued to dream, and without any guidance from the significant adults in her life, her ability to process her perceptions was affected. She became fearful of the fact that she could dream about particular things, and felt confused by her lack of understanding or control of the situation.

The need for adults to take seriously and to listen to what children are saying or hinting at in order to acknowledge their experience is paramount. By doing this, adults – parents, care-givers, educators – might come to see how common such spiritual experiences are. If such a climate of openness can be created, then children may be empowered to tell their stories and to nurture, rather than stifle, the perceptions and sensibilities that they do have.

What can be Learnt from this Research?

There is much that can be learnt from the above research which has sought to explore the spirituality of children. Each of the investigations outlined in this chapter attests to the existence of a spiritual dimension to the lives of children. This dimension exists irrespective of whether or not children belong to a religious tradition, or whether they believe in God. While for some the formal practices of a religious tradition may enable them to give expression to their spirituality, spirituality is not dependent upon religion. Insight into the spirituality of children, as suggested by much of the research, can be gained by focusing on the perceptions, awareness and responses of children to what might be classified as ordinary and everyday activities. This is pertinent for children living in Western secular societies, where the practice of religion is on the decline.

Further, the research explored in this chapter indicates that the spirituality of children is active and can be nurtured if parents and others who work and engage with children have appropriate techniques for respectfully listening to (and for) and acknowledging seriously the individual characteristics of each child's spirituality. In other words, there is a need to honour and listen attentively to the children themselves if insight into their spiritual lives is to be gained.

These investigations also attest to the fact that children are capable of having profound spiritual experiences from an early age. Each child expresses his or her spirituality in different and unique ways, and if this dimension of their lives is not listened to, nurtured and fostered, it can become suppressed and damaged by socially and historically constructed processes. This can lead children, as they grow older, to repress, neglect and even discard the spirituality first experienced in a significant way during childhood. This too is particularly pertinent to children living in Western countries, where the suppression of the spiritual, although a natural predisposition and quality of human life, is an all too real phenomenon.

In a Nutshell

- Contemporary research attests to the existence of a spiritual dimension in the lives of children.

- Children are capable of having profound spiritual experiences from an early age.

- Insight into the spirituality of children can be gained by focusing not only on their use of religious language and concepts, but also on the perceptions, awareness and responses of children to what might be classified as ordinary and everyday activities.

- If the spiritual dimension of children's lives is not listened to, and nurtured, it can become suppressed and damaged by socially and historically constructed processes. This can lead children, as they grow older, to repress, neglect and even discard the spirituality first experienced in a significant way during childhood.

- The spirituality of children is active and can be nurtured if parents and others who work with children have appropriate techniques for respectfully listening to (and for) and acknowledging seriously the individual characteristics of each child's spirituality.

CHAPTER 4

An Approach for Understanding the Expressions of Human Life

As became clear in the previous chapter, expressions of spirituality are in essence expressions of human life, often involving awareness and responses to ordinary, everyday phenomena. As well as indicating this, the research detailed in the previous chapter established a field in which my own investigation could be set. But how does a researcher gain insight into the everyday expressions of children? What type of approach might be adopted in order to come to an understanding of the expressions of human life exhibited by these particular children?

In this chapter I discuss the research design which was adopted for my own investigation. I discuss the theoretical perspective which lay behind the methodology of my study, as well as the more practical details concerning the invitation to children to participate. I also detail the way in which I actually engaged in conversation with these children, and observed their interactions with each other, as well as their responses to the activities which I had planned.

A Qualitative Undertaking

In discussing the research design, perhaps the first point to note is that an investigation of this type, seeking to identify some characteristics of children's spirituality, was not going to be the type of project that would lend itself to large scale statistical analysis and 'number-crunching'. In other words, it was not going to be a quantitative study. Quantitative research understands truth to be an objective reality. Its methods are concerned with the collection of what is considered to be objective and quantifiable data. Such research seeks the attainment of knowledge through method, and through adherence to a set of rules pertaining to a particular method.

However, the 'data' which would form the basis of my study was not going to consist of quantifiable, statistical material. Nor would it necessarily be considered objective – at least, not in a scientific, positivistic sense. It would consist of conversation with small groups of children and observations of them. How does one begin to quantify or measure such information? Further, it was clear that the method used was not going to contain a hard and fast set of rules to guide it, and that my role as a researcher might not necessarily be 'objective' in the scientific sense. As will be discussed later in this chapter, complete objectivity on the part of the researcher is something of a myth.[9] In essence, all of this meant that, rather than being a quantitative study, my investigation was to be situated within a *qualitative* paradigm.

A qualitative study is an enquiry process of coming to understand a human or social problem. It is based on developing a complex and holistic picture using prose, reporting detailed views of the participants, and it is conducted in natural settings rather than in controlled environments (Cresswell 1998). Qualitative research understands reality to be subjective and dimensional as seen by the participants of a particular study. It generally upholds and gives credibility to the collection of thoughts, perceptions and experiences of the participants.

Situated within a qualitative paradigm, my study was underpinned by the notion of constructionism. This holds that all knowledge, and thus all meaningful reality, is contingent upon human practices, and is constructed as the result of the interaction between human beings and their world (Crotty 1998). Whereas objective epistemologies consider truth to be identifiable with precision and certainty, and subjective ones understand truth to be imposed upon the object of research, constructionism maintains that phenomena and their meanings are in the process of continually being constructed by social actors. Knowledge is indeterminate. Social phenomena and their categories are not only fashioned through social interaction, but they are also in a state of constant revision (Bryman 2001).

Important too is that constructionism regards truth as emanating from the relationship between the researcher and the object of the researcher's interest. This understanding is viewed as being central in establishing human beliefs and ideas. It also begins to recognize the importance of the prior understandings the researcher brings to the investigation, thereby dispelling the notion of complete objectivity on the part of the researcher. Therefore, the researcher and object of the researcher's interest emerge as partners in the generation of meaning (Crotty 1998).

Constructionism was integral to my study. The phenomenon under consideration – characteristics of children's spirituality – was such that the identification of these would require my interpretation of the life expressions of the children. Meaning would be generated through my engagement with and reflection upon these life expressions, which were to form the 'texts' of my study. In other words, I, as the researcher, and the life expressions of the children, became partners in the generation of meaning.

Understanding the Expressions of Human Life

If then I, as the researcher, and the life expressions of the children who participated in my study were to become partners in generating meaning, then some theoretical perspective was necessary in order to guide the enquiry. In other words, I needed a theoretical standpoint which would inform an approach for understanding the expressions of human life. Hermeneutic phenomenology provided that impetus.

Hermeneutic phenomenology

The philosophical literature which details hermeneutic phenomenology is abstract and often difficult to comprehend. However, the effort to penetrate it is certainly rewarding, and a number of decisions regarding practical issues can be made by the researcher after reflecting upon the literature on hermeneutic phenomenology. For instance, while many research approaches seek objectivity, hermeneutic phenomenology does not seek to objectify the focus of the researcher's interest. In fact, hermeneutic phenomenology always looks to open up a middle space of deep engagement between the research object and the researcher. Metaphors such as 'play' and 'conversation' are used to describe this middle space.

The hermeneutic phenomenological tradition developed from the work of Edmund Husserl, Martin Heidegger, and particularly Hans-Georg Gadamer.[10] The philosophy underpinning hermeneutic phenomenology is that knowledge is realized in the interpretation and understanding of the expressions of human life (Sharkey 2001). It is a tradition that attempts to be attentive to the way in which things (phenomena) appear to be, and to be interpretive, since all phenomena are encountered meaningfully through lived experience and can be described in human language (van Manen 1990).

PHENOMENOLOGY

Phenomenology is concerned with seeking to provide a true description of an object (phenomenon) based on what the object is in itself. Husserl (1965, first published 1911) was a key figure in the development of phenomenology. Although his method sought to regard an object of a researcher's interest with as few suppositions as possible, Husserl also realized that all understanding is biased according to the perspective of the knower. Genuine understanding is really only ever of aspects of things. This can be likened to the visual limitation of looking at a three-dimensional object. When, for example, a person observes such an object, it is impossible to see it in its entirety. What are visible are partial aspects, seen from different perspectives depending upon where the person is positioned in relation to the object. The disclosure of one aspect, or perspective, necessarily conceals another.

In order to describe such aspects of things, many phenomenologists, such as Canadian scholar Max van Manen, have preferred to say that phenomenological texts need to contain *thickened language* (van Manen 1990), that is, richly descriptive and evocative language that invites the reader to encounter the phenomenon in a new and fresh way. Thickened language has the effect of dispelling the everyday and assumed meanings about the particular phenomenon that is the object of the researcher's interest.

HERMENEUTICS

Primarily, hermeneutics is described as the interpretation of texts, the purpose of which is to arrive at a common understanding of the meaning of a given text (Kvale 1996). It has been in common usage among biblical scholars for the interpretation of scripture. However, Sharkey (2001) has noted that the concept of 'text' has come to be understood more broadly. Texts may refer not only to literary writings and works, but also to a wider range of notions, including discourse, meaningful human action, and even media such as film.

Schwandt (1994) noted that nineteenth century philosopher Wilhelm Dilthey developed his notion of hermeneutics as a counter response to the dominant positivist paradigm of his time. Dilthey argued that although the human sciences – humanities, the arts, and the like – drew upon different methods than those employed in the natural sciences, the human sciences were no less valuable. In essence, his contention was that the modality of the human sciences was concerned with interpreting and understanding the great expressions of human life.

Gadamer (1989, first published in German in 1960) was a key figure in typifying the synthesis that has resulted in hermeneutic phenomenology. There are several insights drawn from the work of Gadamer that have influenced my own research into children's spirituality. These include method, the metaphors of conversation and play as ideals for what ought to occur during the hermeneutical process, understanding as a productive activity, the fusion of horizons, and prior understanding, or as Gadamer terms it, prejudice.

Insights from Gadamer's Work

Method

One of the first things to note is that a researcher who seeks to understand a text, or another's life expression, does not rely on any one particular method in order to do so. Gadamer's work intended to demonstrate the ways in which human understanding both unfolds and is imbedded in human language and history. No one method exists that informs a researcher as to how to inquire into another's life expression. Rather, ascertaining truth is achieved by entering into genuine conversation with the text or life expression. In such a conversation, it is the researcher's powers of observation, reflection and judgment that are brought to the fore.

Conversation

Conversation exemplifies the qualities of responsiveness, creativity and freedom that are central to genuine understanding. A conversation works most effectively when the subject matter of the conversation assumes control, while those in dialogue allow themselves to be led by it. In hermeneutic phenomenology what is sought is a genuine conversation between the researcher, and the life expression, also referred to as the text. As conversation partners, both the researcher and the text contribute to the ebb and flow of the dialogue in valuable, albeit different ways. The text presents insights of value to the researcher, while the latter brings to the text her or his own insights. The text leads the researcher to question her or his own prior understandings, which may be taken for granted (Weinsheimer 1985).

Play

Complementing the notion of conversation is Gadamer's metaphor of play. Both conversation and play express the human capacity for engagement and responsiveness that are to be found at the centre of understanding. Gadamer agued that the playing of a game has the capacity to draw the players into its power, leaving them with no control over its outcome. The whole point of the game is that its conclusion is unknown. It is not clear exactly what will happen – who will win, what a player's next move will be, and so on. Gadamer's reflection highlights that genuine conversation, like play, leads the dialogue partners to become lost in the encounter. The outcome of a genuine conversation, like that of a game, is unknown.

The notion of *middle space* is central to Gadamer's reflection on play and conversation. He suggested that understanding is an event that unfolds in the middle space of encounter between the text, or life expression, and the researcher. Just as the playing of a game is resolved on the playing field, game board, or some other designated space, common meaning between the text and its interpreter is to be found in the encounter between them, that is, in the middle space. Therefore, the researcher who attempts to engage in hermeneutic phenomenology takes seriously the challenge to enter the middle space that is opened up in a playful and dialogical engagement with that which is the object of the researcher's interest.

Understanding as a productive activity

Another Gadamerian insight which influenced my own research is the notion that understanding is a productive activity. Hermeneutical activity always transcends the reproduction of that which may have been an author's original intention. The meaning of a text is co-determined by both the hermeneutic situation of the interpreter, and the horizon projected by the text, or life expression. Because the text must necessarily always be understood from within the particular context of the interpreter, the activity of interpretation cannot be one of simply reproducing whatever may have been in the mind of the author. Rather, the hermeneutic process is a productive activity. The meaning of a life expression, or text, must be co-determined by the particularity of the interpreter and the text itself.

This is not to imply that texts can have a multiplicity of meanings attached to them by anyone and everyone who would seek to interpret them. Gadamer's assertion is rather that there does not exist one 'ready made' meaning which lies in wait of an interpreter. Understanding is the result of interpretation that is co-determined by the hermeneutic situation of all involved.

Nor is this to imply that hermeneutic phenomenological research results in a work of fiction. As a productive activity, such writing involves the use of thickened language (van Manen 1990) that seeks to evoke the underlying essence of the phenomenon as the researcher has encountered it. It seeks to invite the reader to enter the world which the text has revealed and so encounter the phenomenon in a new and fresh way.

Fusion of horizons

Of particular influence in my own research was Gadamer's notion of understanding as a fusion of horizons. A horizon marks the limit of everything that can be understood from a particular point of view. However, it is possible for a person to see beyond an immediate standpoint. Therefore, an individual's horizon of understanding is constantly in the process of formation. It is not something that remains static.

For Gadamer, understanding occurs when the horizon projected by the life expression, or text, combines with the researcher's own comprehension and interpretive insight. It can be likened to a conversation, where what is expressed is common to both of the conversation partners. In hermeneutic phenomenological research, what is produced as the result of the investigation is something which is of value and insight that is common to both the researcher and the life expression.

While it is true that hermeneutic phenomenological research seeks to be faithful to the text and the horizon projected by it, such an activity is, in itself, incomplete. For Gadamer, this would amount to little more than simply reconstructing that which may have been in the mind of the author of the text. Hermeneutic phenomenological research must also take into account the particularities, insights, and prior understandings of the researcher. In this way, the particularities and prior understandings of the researcher fuse with those of the text to produce something which is both new and common to both.

Prior understanding (prejudice)

As alluded to above, in hermeneutic phenomenology, prior understanding plays an important role. While many research approaches attempt to eliminate the prior understandings of the investigator, hermeneutic phenomenological research views prior understanding as a prerequisite for any act of interpretation. Gadamer called these 'prejudices', and argued that these gave the hermeneutic problem its real thrust. The goal is not to eliminate these prejudices, but rather to test them through engagement with the life expression or text. In his commentaries upon the work of Gadamer, Weinsheimer (1985) argued that the interpreter needs to place her or his prejudices at risk. The text is needed as a means by which to highlight the dubiousness of what the interpreter takes for granted. In this way, new possibilities for questioning and extending the interpreter's own horizon of understanding are disclosed. So, not only is complete objectivity on the part of the researcher impossible, in hermeneutic phenomenology, a researcher's prior understandings are considered to be important. They are not to be eliminated, but rather, they comprise a pivotal necessity for the hermeneutic problem.

These insights guided my own research into the characteristics of children's spirituality. Through my investigation, the 'data' collected were the life expressions of the children who participated in my research, consisting of both conversation and observation. In keeping with the hermeneutic phenomenological tradition, I have referred to this data as the texts, or life expressions, of my study. In the next section of this chapter I describe how I collected these life expressions – the texts – of my study. But the point I wish to make here is that in analyzing these texts, I attempted to enter into conversation with them, and to produce something of meaning as the result of the fusion of my own horizon of understanding with that of the texts. In other words, the understanding which resulted was productive, and co-determined by the contexts of myself as the researcher and the life expressions of the children.

The Research Process

After seeking permission from the appropriate authorities, three Catholic primary schools, one in each of three settings – inner city, suburban and rural – were invited to take part in my study by allowing, in consultation with the head teacher and parents, children from their school community to meet with me. The fact that Catholic schools were selected rather than public schools reflected the context in which I as the researcher was working. I was employed at a Catholic university which, although publicly funded, had close affiliations with Catholic schools through its field experience programmes for undergraduate pre-service teachers. The Catholic Education Office in Melbourne, one of the authorities from whom I sought permission to conduct the research, was also both supportive of the study and interested in the findings of the investigation in terms of how they might impact on Catholic schools. However, while my study was limited to some children in Catholic schools, and not designed to make broad generalizations (as is the case with quantitative research), my findings were consistent with, and reflect the results of other studies which explored the spirituality of children in other settings (for example, Champagne 2003; Erricker *et al.* 1997; Hay and Nye 2006; Moriarty 2007). This will become apparent in later chapters.

A total of 36 children were to be indiscriminately invited to participate in my study. This total was to be made up of 12 children from each of the three schools: six children in Year 3 (approximately eight years of age) and six in Year 5 (approximately ten years of age). This total was comparable to the total numbers of children who participated in other qualitative studies investigating aspects of children's spirituality (for example, Adams 2001, 2003; Halstead and Waite 2001; Reimer and Furrow 2001). The particular year levels were chosen because it was felt that children of ages eight and ten respectively would be able to engage in the type of conversation and activity that I had planned.

It was hoped that there would be a balance of male and female participants. Letters were sent to the parents of all children in these year levels in all three schools, outlining the purpose of the research and seeking permission to allow their children to participate. As a researcher, I spent one two-hour session each week over a period of five weeks in each of the classrooms from which the children were drawn, observing and assisting the classroom teacher. This prolonged engagement (Lincoln and Guba 1985) was useful in helping to ensure that I was not encountered as a total stranger when interacting with these children during the research. It helped to build a sense of familiarity and trust with me. At the conclusion of this five-week period in each school, small groups of six were indiscriminately selected from those whose parents had given permission for them to participate.

I chose to meet with groups of children rather than individually for two reasons. First, in being guided by the work of Halstead and Waite (2001) and McCreery (1996), I felt that the group dynamic may have been beneficial in enabling children to feel less threatened and more comfortable in the company of their peers. The conversation that I planned was being geared to group participation. I also wanted the children to engage in some activities which, to a large extent, I felt allowed for group dialogue.

The second reason for meeting with groups of children was a practical one concerning the issue of a protective safeguard for both myself and the children. Given a number of events, all of which were recent at the time I was conducting the research, and which had been made public by the media concerning the abuse of trust by those in positions of authority, I felt it inappropriate to meet with children on an individual basis. So, despite the possible disadvantages concerning meeting with groups, including the fact that some of the children may have been reluctant to speak in the company of their peers for fear of ridicule, I decided to meet with groups of children rather than individuals.

Three semi-structured meetings with each group of children in each of the three schools were subsequently planned. Each meeting included two phases, both guided by one of the three interrelating categories of spiritual sensitivity outlined by Hay and Nye (2006) – awareness sensing, mystery sensing, and value sensing. The first phase consisted of a short story, some guiding questions and conversation loosely structured around one of these three categories. The second phase consisted of an activity, again guided by one of these categories of spiritual sensitivity. While I acknowledge that each of these categories is interrelated, one such type became the focus for each group meeting.

Awareness sensing was the focus of the first group meeting. Awareness sensing involves attending to the here and now of experience, the total engagement in a particular activity and the alertness to what might be experienced in moments of stillness or concentration. In order to evoke this sense of awareness, the children were invited to select from a variety of activities that may have involved attending to the present moment of experience. These activities included jigsaw puzzles, 'bead creations', drawing, and seed planting.

The focus of the second group meeting was mystery sensing. This involves the wonder and awe, the fascination and questioning that is characteristic of children as they interact with their world. In order to evoke this sense of mystery, an ambiance was created by playing a Nature Soundscape CD – Tony O'Connor's *Uluru* (1999). Also, an oil burner was used, and an essential oil – eucalyptus – was burnt. I envisaged that these might draw upon the children's sense of smell and hearing in evoking a sense of mystery. The children were invited to talk about and discuss one or more of a set of photographs, similar to the types of pictures used by Hay and Nye (2006) in their conversations with children.

Value sensing was the focus of the third group meeting. Value sensing concerns the moral sensitivity of children. It includes a sense of that which really matters to them. In order to evoke this sense of value, the children were invited to respond to the reflection 'I wonder what you think really, really matters?' (Rebecca Nye, personal communication, 9 May 2002). This question implicitly asked what it was that was of ultimate value or concern for these children, and so addressed their search for meaning. I also asked a second related question, 'If you could have three wishes, I wonder what you might wish for?' As well as responding verbally to these question, the children were also invited to record their responses and, if they felt comfortable in doing so, to allow me to have access to their journal entries.

This was an ethically sensitive moment in the conducting of the research, and care needed to be exercised in addressing the dynamic of the adult–child relationship. In attending to this aspect, I decided to indicate to the children prior to them beginning the task that they would be invited to allow me to view their journals. The notion of this being an invitation was emphasized so that, if the children so wished, they could refuse this invitation.

The length of time planned for each meeting varied due to the nature of the activity planned for phase two. However, it was envisaged that each group meeting would have a duration of between half an hour and 45 minutes. In practice, some of the meetings ran for nearly an hour.

Each of the three meetings was recorded using videotape. This had two particular advantages. First, it recorded the conversation and discussion with the children which, when viewed and reflected upon, may have provided insight into their verbalized expressions of spirituality. But, second, and in some instances most importantly, it provided a means by which to capture and interpret what was not articulated – their facial expressions, body language, interaction with one another during the activities, and their silences. These would provide me with a more holistic picture – a more complete text, or life expression – upon which I could reflect, and which may have revealed different aspects of their spirituality.

The Schools and Participants

The suburban school invited to participate in this study was situated approximately 15 kilometres from the city centre of Melbourne. There were approximately 280 students enrolled during the time of the research. These students came from predominately middle-class, Anglo-European families.

A total of 12 children – five boys and seven girls – took part in the study from this school. The following names of the children who participated have been fictionalized in order to protect their identity. From the Year 3 class, the children with whom I met were Joseph, Stacey, Sally, Emma, Milly, Zephania and Eloise. The children from the Year 5 class were Adam, Cameron, Danny, John and Alicia.

The inner city school invited to participate in this study was situated approximately three kilometres from the city centre of Melbourne. At the time of my visit there were approximately 150 students enrolled from a variety of multicultural and multi-faith backgrounds. Among the cultural groups represented in the school were Vietnamese, North African, Lebanese, Egyptian and Iraqi. The religious backgrounds of the children included Catholic, Eastern Maronite and Chaldean Catholic rites, as well as children from Muslim, Buddhist and Hindu faith traditions.

A total of 12 children – six boys and six girls – took part in the group meetings. Their names (again fictionalized) were Marco, Tran, Amina, Charlotte, Ali and Rosie from the Year 3 class, and May Ling, Missal, Hy Sun, Fadde, Maria and Ramsey from the Year 5 class.

The rural school invited to participate in this study was located approximately 150 kilometres east from the city centre of Melbourne. It was situated in a tightly knit community surrounded by mountain ranges. At the time of my visit there were approximately 110 students enrolled, emanating from farming families. While the majority of the students were from Anglo-Celtic backgrounds, a large number came from families who were Christian, but not Catholic, and many came from families who professed to have no particular religious affiliation.

There were 11 children – four boys and seven girls – who participated from this school. The fictionalized names of the children from the Year 3 class were Susan, Imelda, Michael, Wallace and Tom. The names of the students from the Year 5 class, again, fictionalized, were Lara, James, Kristy, Annabelle, Michelle and Emily.

Although it was intended that there be 36 participants, in total, there were 35 children who, with their parents' permission, took part in this research – 15 boys and 20 girls. For the most part, all of the named children met with me in each of the group meetings. In some instances, due to absence because of illness and the like, not all of the children were present at school on each of the days the group meetings were conducted.

Rehearsing and Preparing the Ground

Having decided upon the format for each of the three meetings, having formulated an interview guide, and selected appropriate activities in which the children would engage, I was then faced with the task of determining whether what I had planned would enable me to gain insight into these children's spirituality. In a quantitative investigation, I might have conducted a pilot study to determine the effectiveness of my approach. However, in keeping with the hermeneutic phenomenological tradition, I rather set about preparing the ground for my research. My task was then to rehearse one of the three meetings with one group of children. It was impractical, and too time consuming I felt, to rehearse each of the three meetings, as well as placing additional pressure on the school communities, who were kind enough to allow me to conduct the research in their schools. Therefore I selected one group of children in Year 5 in one of the three schools and rehearsed the interview guide and planned activities for the awareness sensing meeting with them.

This rehearsal would prepare the ground for the research. It would provide me with some initial indications as to whether the semi-structured interview might generate the sort of conversation that would enable me to gain insight into the spirituality of these children. Through this, I was able to practise interacting with the children, probing where necessary for further information, or remaining silent to allow the children's voices to be heard, and to enable them to elaborate in their own terms. I was also able to decide whether or not the planned activities were appropriate for observing. The rehearsal also enabled me to determine the optimum positioning of the video camera so as to capture not only conversation, but the children's reactions, body languages, facial gestures, silences and engagement in the planned activities. This crucial aspect would ultimately determine the quality of the text for reflecting upon and interpreting.

As a result of the rehearsal, it became clear that the children, in this particular group at least, were more than willing to enter into conversation with me. They generated much valuable discussion, and it became clear that my planned interview guide was exactly that – a guide! The children themselves, for the most part, were really in control of the direction of the discussion. This needed to be so if I was to hear and experience anything of their spirituality. In light of this, I made only minimal changes to the interview guide. The questions and discussion starters I had planned seemed to provide enough stimuli to generate discussion. While it could not be guaranteed that this would be the case for every group of children, I was prepared to make judgments based on this initial experience.

Lifeworld Existentials as Guides to Reflection

Having collected the texts – the life expressions of these children – the question arose as to how I would actually analyze them. Through what lenses would I interpret their expressions? Since my study took its theoretical impetus from hermeneutic phenomenology, I drew upon van Manen's (1990) notion of lifeworld existentials as guides to reflection and interpretation of the texts. In the phenomenological literature, the lifeworld existentials have been well utilized and have been seen as fundamentally belonging to the structure of people's lived experience (see for example Heidegger 1980, first published in

German in 1927; Merleau-Ponty 1996, first published in French in 1945). I also have previously drawn upon these lifeworld existentials in reflecting upon children's life expressions (Hyde 2003b, 2005). There are four lifeworld existentials that permeate the lived experiences of all human beings, regardless of their social, cultural or historical contexts: lived space (spatiality), lived body (corporeality), lived time (temporality), and lived human relations (relationality).

Lived space refers to felt space. When thinking of space, we commonly think of geometrical space, that is the dimensions of space – height, length, depth and so forth. However, lived space refers to the landscape in which people move and in which they consider themselves at home (van Manen 1990). It is helpful to inquire into the nature of the lived space that may render a particular experience or phenomena its quality of meaning. For example, the reading of a book may entail a space that is conducive to reading – a quiet corner, a comfortable chair, a table in a secluded coffee shop or book room.[11]

Lived body refers to the phenomenological fact that human beings are always literally situated bodily in the world. When people encounter one another in the lifeworld, they do so through bodily presence – a handshake, an embrace, a gaze, a smile, and so forth (van Manen 1990). In this physical bodily presence something is both revealed and concealed simultaneously. For example, when a person is the object of someone else's gaze, her or his modality of being may be enhanced, such as when two lovers gaze at each other.

Lived time is the time that seems to speed up in enjoyment, and slow down in periods of boredom or anxiousness. It is the human being's temporal way of being in the world. Van Manen (1990) maintained that the temporal dimensions of past, present and future in fact comprise the horizons of a person's temporal landscape. As a person's identity emerges, she or he not only lives towards a future that is taking shape, but also reinterprets the past in light of who she or he has now become. The past changes because a person lives towards a future which is beginning to take shape.

Lived human relation refers to the relationships people maintain with others in the interpersonal space they share. When people encounter one another, they do so in a corporeal way. They are able to develop a conversational relation with the other. In the larger existential sense, human beings have always searched in their experience of the Other for a sense of life's meaning and purpose. Tacey (2003) maintained that the Self only comes to know itself in relationship with the Other. Without an absolute Other, the Self lacks a sense of identity, definition and form. Therefore, in a religious sense, many have searched in their experience of, and in relation to the Transcendent for a sense of identity and life's meaning and purpose. Some would name the Transcendent, the ultimate ground of being, as God.

Van Manen (1990) maintained that these four lifeworld existentials can be differentiated, but not separated. In a study such as mine, the existentials may be studied in their differentiated aspects, while acknowledging that each existential calls forth the others. In this study, these four lifeworld existentials became the lenses through which the texts were interpreted.

My Reflective Journal

The means by which I was able to reflect upon the life expressions of the children in my study – the videotaped group meetings – was through the use of a reflective journal. After viewing each of the videotaped group meetings many times over, I wrote descriptive hermeneutic phenomenological reflections woven around each of the four lifeworld existentials, for those videoed sections which seemed to suggest that these children's spirituality was being expressed (or in some cases, sections where such expression seemed to be inhibited). These contained thickened language that sought to describe what the children had to say in conversation, as well as their reactions, silences and body language during the group meetings. The descriptions attempted to capture the presence of the phenomenon – their spirituality – in a new and fresh way.

The Credibility of the Research

My study was to be situated within a qualitative paradigm, which understands reality to be subjective and dimensional as seen by the participants of a particular study. It generally upholds and gives credibility to the collection of thoughts, perceptions and experiences of the participants. This being the case, questions arose in relation to how I would be able to assure the quality of my research. In quantitative work, which usually involves the objective collection of data that can be quantified in some way, researchers use the concepts of reliability and validity to evaluate the quality of their work. However, and as discussed earlier in this chapter, in my study, my role as the researcher was not, in a positivistic sense, objective. Apart from the fact total objectivity on the part of the researcher is virtually impossible, the type of research in which I was engaged relied upon my prior understandings (prejudices) in order to give the investigation its real thrust. Therefore, I would need to find other means by which to persuade others that the findings of my inquiry were worth paying attention to, and were worthy of being taken into account.

Lincoln and Guba (1985) have argued that in qualitative research, it is the *trustworthiness* of the inquiry that needs to be established. They have proposed four criteria as being suitable for establishing the trustworthiness of such inquiry – credibility, transferability, dependability, and confirmability. Outlined briefly below are the ways in which I addressed each of these criteria in my study.

Credibility

Credibility was addressed through the notions of prolonged engagement and persistent observation (Lincoln and Guba 1985). Prolonged engagement refers to the investment of sufficient time in becoming oriented to the context or research site, and also to the notion of building trust with the research participants. I achieved this by spending one two-hour session each week over a period of five weeks in each of the classrooms from which the children were drawn. This enabled me to become oriented to the classroom contexts from which these children came. Prolonged engagement also enabled me to establish a rapport and to build trust with the children. The building of trust is both a time consuming and developmental process, yet essential if adequate trust and rapport are to emerge between the researcher and the participants.

The notion of persistent observation also helped to establish the credibility of this study. Persistent observation involves attending to the salient factors of the phenomenon under consideration. It entails the ability to identify those characteristics and elements of a situation that are most relevant to the research, and to focus on these in detail. It also involves a sorting out of the irrelevancies – those elements that do not really count. In my study, persistent observation was undertaken particularly in relation to the viewing and reviewing of the texts – the videotaped group meetings, and to the recordings made in the reflective journal. It involved me in the process of sorting out of both relevancies and irrelevancies. This was often challenging, as there was considerable information gathered through the videotaping process.

Transferability

Within a qualitative paradigm, the perception of transferability is different to the way in which it might be understood within a positivist approach that relies on external validity. Within a qualitative paradigm, transferability depends on context. But whether the findings hold in some other context, or even in the same context at some other time, is an empirical, not a qualitative issue.

Transferability was addressed in my study through the detailed reflections and interpretations of the texts of this study, resulting in the use of thickened language (van Manen 1990) to describe the features and characteristics of the children's spirituality. These hermeneutic phenomenological descriptions and reflections were recorded in my reflective journal, extracts of which are included in the following chapters. These may potentially enable the reader to encounter the phenomenon of spirituality in a new and fresh way. Lincoln and Guba (1985) have argued that although such descriptions do not specify the external validity of an inquiry, they do in fact enable others interested in replicating the research to reach a conclusion about whether such a transfer might be considered as a possibility.

Dependability

Lincoln and Guba (1985) have argued that there can be no dependability without credibility. That is, a demonstration of the credibility of the research is sufficient to establish its dependability. While such an assertion has merit, and may establish dependability in principle, I was eager to demonstrate dependability in practice.

Accordingly, dependability was also addressed in my study through ensuring that all phases of the research were accurately described and documented. The videotaping of each group meeting also assisted in ensuring dependability. Although I was the only person to view these recordings, the videotapes formed the texts for reflection and interpretation. As such they were viewed many times to ensure that the conversation (Gadamer1989) between the text and the interpreter was genuine, and that the understandings of each were weighed and tested throughout this conversation.

Confirmability

Confirmability was addressed in my study firstly through the reflective journal in which were recorded the hermeneutic phenomenological descriptions and reflections upon the texts under consideration. Confirmability was further addressed by my academic colleagues at Australian Catholic University, who assisted in confirming that, while absolute objectivity is impossible in any research (Bryman 2001), I made a conscious attempt not to allow personal values and judgments, or theoretical inclinations, to overtly influence the conduct of the research and findings that evolved from it. That is, they helped to ensure that my prior understandings and prejudices were tested by the life expressions of the participants, and brought into conversation with them. They were also able to confirm that I remained faithful to the philosophical underpinnings of hermeneutic phenomenology.

In a Nutshell

- The research approach I adopted was situated within a qualitative paradigm, which understands reality to be subjective and dimensional as seen by the participants of a particular study. It generally upholds and gives credibility to the collection of thoughts, perceptions and experiences of the participants.

- Hermeneutic phenomenology was used as the theoretical standpoint for reflecting on and gaining insight into the spirituality of children in my study.

- Three schools were invited to take part in my study – one in an inner city location, one in a suburban location, one in a rural location.

- A total of 35 children participated in my research. This total was made up of two groups of about six children in each of the three schools – one group at Year 3 (children approximately eight years of age), and one group at Year 5 (children approximately ten years of age).

- I met with each group of children three times, with each meeting lasting for about 45 minutes, although in some instances, the meetings lasted for about an hour.

- Each of the group meetings was guided by one of the categories of spiritual sensitivity as outlined by Hay and Nye (2006): awareness sensing, mystery sensing, and value sensing.

- Each group meeting was videotaped, so as to capture the life expressions of the children. This enabled me to reflect upon not only what was said, but also on that which was not said – body language, facial expressions, silences, etc.

- I employed van Manen's (1990) lifeworld existentials as guides to reflection upon the life expressions of these children as a means by which to gain insight into their spirituality.

- The criteria of credibility, transferability, dependability, and confirmability were used to establish the trustworthiness of my inquiry.

PART 2

The Characteristics
of Children's Spirituality

A Preface to Part 2

In the previous chapters, the focus has been on preparing the ground for investigating the characteristics of children's spirituality. Those chapters discussed my conceptual understanding of the word 'spirituality', previous research which has sought to identify various aspects of children's spirituality, and the approach that I adopted for my research design.

The following chapters centre on the characteristics of children's spirituality which I have discerned through my research. These have been gleaned as the result of hermeneutic phenomenological reflection upon the texts of my study – the videotaped conversations and observations of each group meeting – through the reflective journal. Each group meeting took as its focus one the categories of spiritual sensitivity described by Hay and Nye (2006) – awareness sensing, mystery sensing and value sensing. The following chapters, 5 through to 8, explore the characteristics of spirituality that were discerned in relation to these categories.

In general, much discussion and dialogue took place during each of the group meetings. The children's discussion centred on a wide range of topics which, as well as including the focus for each group meeting, incorporated their likes and dislikes, what they did on the weekend, their favourite foods and hobbies, their football teams and sporting achievements, their favourite school subjects, as well as sharing with me the composition of their friendship groups and families and their pets. In brief, the children talked about their engagement with the everyday. While the videotaped group meetings contained numerous possible characteristics which may have been indicative of these children's spirituality, there were four characteristics which, as the result of a thorough reflection upon the recordings, emerged consistently among each group of children in each of the three school locations. I am not suggesting that these children's spirituality was limited to these four characteristics, nor am I suggesting that other characteristics were not possible. However, as these particular four characteristics appeared to be evident across each group, they have become the focus of the following chapters.

The process I employed, as noted in Chapter 4, involved viewing and reviewing, several times, each of the videotaped recordings – the texts – of the group meetings. Notes were made in my reflective journal in relation to the similarities which seemed to be recurring in each of the texts. I then 'bookmarked' each section of each of the group meetings in which there was evidence suggesting the presence of a particular characteristic of the children's spirituality for further viewing and reflection at a later date. These particular bookmarked sections were then viewed again – several times – and additional notes made in my reflective journal, along with some verbatim transcriptions of the children's words, body language, facial expressions, silences, and the like.

In this section of the book, each characteristic that has been discerned is presented and outlined, with some hermeneutic phenomenological descriptions of the texts that exemplify the presence of the particular characteristic. I have been selective in the inclusion of these texts. To include every possible example would have proved impractical. Instead, I have incorporated examples of those texts which seemed to me to clearly indicate the presence of each of the particular characteristics. Following the texts indicative of each particular characteristic, I have included a reflection and discussion woven around van Manen's (1990) lifeworld existentials – lived body, lived time, lived space, and lived relation. Rather than taking each of these existential lenses separately, each reflection attempts to integrate them into a coherent whole, since one cannot be isolated from the others. Each calls forth the other aspects as they are interconnected.

Following this, I have included some guidelines for parents, teachers, and others who may work with children in various capacities, in relation to how each of these particular characteristics of children's spirituality might be nurtured. The suggestions included are certainly not exhaustive. In fact it is hoped that by considering those I have offered, the reader might discern other ideas for nurturing each of the particular characteristics of children's spirituality that I have identified.

The four characteristics of the children's spirituality which were identified as the result of such a reflection were:

1. the felt sense

2. integrating awareness

3. weaving the threads of meaning, and

4. spiritual questing.

There were two factors also identified that appeared to inhibit these children's expression of their spirituality. These have been termed *material pursuit* and *trivializing*. While there were potentially other factors that may have inhibited these children's expression of their spirituality, these two particular factors, once again, showed a degree of consistency across the groups of children who participated in this study. The discernment of these two factors occurred through the process described above for the identification of the characteristics of children's spirituality. These two inhibiting factors are presented and discussed in Chapter 9.

Again, I have included some guidelines for parents, teachers, and others who may work with children in various capacities, in relation to counteracting these particular factors that act in a destructive way upon children's expression of their spirituality. The suggestions may provide a valuable stimulus for discussion among groups of parents and among professionals who have an interest in promoting and cultivating the spiritual dimension of childhood.

As discussed in Chapter 4, where I described my approach for studying the expressions of human life, the names of the children in all instances have been fictionalized in order to protect their identities.

CHAPTER 5

The Felt Sense

In this chapter I discuss the first of the characteristics identified in my research. I have termed this characteristic 'the felt sense'.[12] It became evident during the first meeting with each group of children, which took as its focus the concept of awareness sensing (Hay and Nye 2006). Awareness sensing involves attending to the here and now of experience, the total engagement in a particular activity, and the alertness to what might be experienced in moments of concentration and stillness. After some initial conversation centred on times when they may have been completely absorbed in an activity so as to be attending to the present moment of their experiences, the children were invited to select from a variety of activities that may have involved attending to the here and now of experience. These activities included seed planting, bead creations, jigsaw puzzles, and drawing.

Initially, my engagement with the life expressions of these children in the awareness sensing group meetings led me to recognize an attribute described by American psychologist Mihaly Csikszentmihalyi (1975, 1990) as *flow*. Csikszentmihalyi (1975) described flow as the feeling one might have when, for example, one reads a compelling book, or becomes lost in a fascinating conversation. Flow is an holistic sensation that a person may feel when acting with total involvement. Csikszentmihalyi suggests that in flow, action follows upon action according to an interior logic that seems to require no conscious intervention by the individual. The person experiences it as a unified flowing from one moment to the next. Although in control of her or his actions, little, if any, distinction is experienced between self and environment, and between the past, present and future. In this way, flow involves the experience of concentrated attention giving way to a liberating feeling of the activity being managed by itself, or by some outside influence. From Csikszentmihalyi's description, the action of the activity in which one is involved and the awareness of that activity become merged.

Typical activities that might result in an experience of flow include music, art, yoga, the martial arts, games, rock climbing, and even a person's work when satisfaction is derived from it. Religious ritual too can be a source of flow for an individual. For example, the Jesuit Rule and the spiritual exercises devised by Ignatius of Loyola can be understood as an attempt to generate the experience of flow. In the focused attention to the act of one's breathing, for instance, Hay and Nye (2006) note that such exercises potentially provided the most advantageous set of conditions by which men could live the entirety of their lives as a single flow experience. This is not dissimilar to the Eastern tradition of *vipassana* (awareness meditation) in Theravada Buddhism.

Although I did not explicitly use the term *flow* with the children, they were introduced to this concept through the telling of a story as a part of the first phase of the awareness sensing group meetings. In all of these meetings the children were able to recall occasions on which, in essence, they had apperceived an experience of flow. For example, John in Year 5 from the sub-urban school stated:

> I was playing with my sister's birthday present. It was a little
> bead-threading thing, and you had to look so closely at it that you
> couldn't pay attention to anything else. It wasn't until I dropped a bead
> that I realized that mum was calling me for lunch.

Similarly, May Ling in Year 5 from the inner city school recounted the following:

> Once, when I was lining up at the end of lunch time, I was looking at a
> bird on the ground not far from me. I think it was a sparrow, because it
> was really little. The teacher must have called for us to walk into class, but
> I was still looking at the bird. My back was turned away from the teacher
> and I didn't realize that my line had moved, and suddenly I was standing
> by myself.

Wallace, a Year 3 student in the rural school recalled the following:

> I'm a computer freak and every time I'm fixed on something, everything
> turns to total blackness except for me and the thing I'm fixed on.
> Everything disappears, and only me and the thing I'm fixed on are there.
> Like, nothing else exists.

While Csikszentmihalyi's notion of flow is helpful in describing what appeared to be occurring, it became apparent through the awareness sensing group meetings that something more than flow was being displayed by these children when they engaged in the activities that I had planned. Although the above descriptions offered by the children were indicative of flow, in reflecting upon the texts of this study it became clear that the children's expression of flow could be further characterized by two distinctive features. The first of these is the focus for this chapter, and has been termed the felt sense.

The Felt Sense

Attending to the felt sense entails Hay and Nye's (2006) notion of the here and now of experience. It refers to the intensity and immediacy of awareness of the present moment. In attending to the felt sense, an individual may become lost in the activity in which she or he is engaged. A lack of awareness in relation to the passing of time seemed to be common in such an experience among these children. Further, these experiences tend (although not always) to be private. They are experienced only by the individual. The following reflective journal entry on the Year 5 suburban school children is indicative of this:

> The children proceeded to their selected activity. Adam headed for the seed planting, the materials of which were located on one of the tables. Alicia, John and Cameron made their way to the table containing the materials for the bead creations. Although the three children sat next to one other, there was no interaction among them. They could well have been physically situated in separate countries, or at opposite ends of the earth, for there appeared no dealings among them. Each was engaged and focused on her or his own activity…although they were seated within close proximity to one another, each seemed to be oblivious to the presence of her or his peers.

Of particular relevance in attending to the felt sense is a notion presented by American psychotherapist Eugene Gendlin, called *focusing*. Focusing involves attending to the bodily awareness of situations, persons, or events. Bodily awareness, as Gendlin (1981) has maintained, is not a mental experience, but a *physical* one. It doesn't come in the form of thoughts, words, or other separate components, but as a single, though sometimes puzzling and complex, bodily feeling. It doesn't communicate itself in words, and so is difficult to describe. It is a deep-down level of awareness.

Gendlin argued that people encounter and act upon the world with the whole of their bodies. A person's corporeality is a primary source of knowledge, although it is a source that Western culture tends to discard in favour of the intellect. Attending to this source of knowledge may enable a person to draw upon the wisdom of the body in assisting with personal difficulties and in being sensitively aware in relationships. That is to say, it may enable an individual to get in touch with the felt sense of a particular situation. The following reflective journal entry on one of the Year 5 children from the suburban school is indicative of this feature of the felt sense:

> Adam carefully and skillfully engaged in the tactile experience of placing potting mix into the seed boxes. He seemed to acknowledge the texture and consistency of the soil by rubbing it between his finger tips and thumb before patting it into each of the sockets. Then, delicately, he placed one or two of the seeds into each of the sockets, and gently compressed them into the potting mixture. In a way that could almost be described as lovingly, he added a little water to each.

Similarly, two of the children in Year 3 from the inner city school exhibited this quality of the felt sense:

> Marco headed straight for the bead creations activity. He selected his stencil and began to choose beads to place on it. 'I'm going to finish this,' he murmured almost to himself as he settled and began to engage in this activity. His focus was almost immediate. Carefully and skillfully, he manipulated the beads, selecting his colours and moving them into position. His actions and awareness seemed to merge as a look of delight came across his face.
>
> Soon, he was joined by Tran (who also) began to engage in this activity. Quite consciously and gently, Tran deliberately ran his fingers across the pile of beads, acknowledging their texture and shape. He selected his beads with thought and care.
>
> 'Oh no,' whispered Marco. He had accidentally knocked some of the beads from their position on the stencil. Painstakingly, he set about restoring his work... One might intuit a reverence – almost a sense of the sacred in this activity. It was as though both children desired to maintain the silence and tranquility of the space in which this activity was undertaken, and which this activity seemed to deserve.

A group of girls in Year 5 from the rural school also exhibited this particular quality of the felt sense as they worked cooperatively on the jigsaw activity:

> Kristy's finger tips gently ran across the individual pieces that were laid out on the floor, searching for the correct interlocking parts. There seemed a need and a desire to honor the quiet – the sacredness – that this activity required... (as other children joined her) their finger tips seemed to caress the individual jigsaw pieces, almost as if to 'get a feel' for the right piece. It was almost as if the resulting bodily sensation would somehow indicate the correct piece that might be required in order to complete their section. Although they were using their sense of sight to search the array of

patterns presented by the jigsaw pieces, they seemed to be relying on the wisdom of their sense of touch to guide them in locating the required pieces in order to attempt and complete this particular task.

With the arms and hands of the different children moving across one another, and in and out of each other's way, there was a sense in which a communal space had been created for the completion of this activity. They worked together with purpose... It was not long before various sections that were being completed were ready to be attached to the original larger segment. There was some excitement as this was undertaken, accompanied by looks of pride and satisfaction.

My announcement that they had been working for almost half an hour and that it was almost time to conclude was met with cries of surprise and disappointment. 'Oh no!' they lamented as one voice. They had been so focused upon their task that they seemed genuinely surprised that some 30 minutes of time had passed.

The felt sense, as a characteristic of children's spirituality identified in my study, entailed the attending to physical bodily awareness on the part of the individual. Each child's corporeality seemed to act as a primal source of knowledge which enabled them to draw upon their own bodily wisdom as a means by which to get in touch with the felt sense of a particular situation.

A Reflection and Discussion on the Felt Sense

A conscious perception of physical bodily awareness

The children in my study encountered the various activities in which they chose to engage – seed planting, 'bead creations', jigsaw puzzles, and drawing/painting – in a corporeal way. In attending to each of these tactile activities, the children's felt sense seemed to involve a conscious perception of physical bodily awareness. In other words, the children appeared to be fully aware of their bodily engagement with the activity of their choice. When planting his seeds, Adam manipulated the soil between the tips of his fingers and his thumb, acknowledging the texture and consistency of the potting mix. He gently compressed the seeds into the soil mixture and watered them. All of this was undertaken consciously and deliberately. Adam's perception of, as well as his sensorial and bodily interaction with the materials involved in the seed planting activity, led to his conscious thinking and acting upon the task. In other words, his whole Self was acting upon the task.

While engaged in the 'bead creations' activity, Tran consciously and deliberately ran his fingers across the pile of beads, selecting his colours and positioning these beads with care. Marco painstakingly set about restoring his work after he had accidentally knocked some of the beads from their position on the template. Although oblivious to the presence of the other children around them, Tran and Marco seemed quite conscious of their own engagement in the task, and of their own senses acting upon the task. In both instances, these two children's conscious thinking and acting upon the tasks led to their whole and total involvement in the task. In other words, their whole Selves were acting upon the task.

Similarly, in completing the jigsaw puzzle, Kristy appeared to be consciously moving her fingertips across the jigsaw pieces that were spread out on the floor, almost as if the bodily sensation resulting from this would somehow indicate the correct piece needed to complete a particular section of the puzzle. Although she used her sense of sight to search the array of patterns in front of her, she seemed to be relying on the intuition and wisdom of physical sensation inherent in her sense of touch and shape to find the pieces needed to finish the jigsaw. Intuitively, she seemed to know what she was doing. Her actions appeared to be instinctive and seemed to be the result of the interaction between her senses of sight and touch, as well as her thinking about the process in which she was involved. In other words, she was drawing upon and relying upon the wisdom of her own body (Gendlin 1981).

These conscious bodily experiences seem to be closely linked with Thomas Merton's notion of becoming unified with Other, as discussed in Chapter 2. This becomes particularly apparent in relation to his concept of ontological awareness (Del Prete 2002). For Merton, an ontological way of knowing is a natural predisposition of humankind, although it is one that is largely neglected in Western culture. Ontological awareness is the ability to perceive with one's whole Self – one's whole being – in a direct, experiential and concrete way. In such a way of knowing, a person enters the realm of holistic experience. The whole of the individual is involved – mind, body and soul – without distinction or separation, as well as the whole of the experience in which the person is engaged. This stands in contrast to the scholastic, Aristotelian philosophy that has held sway in the West. Such a philosophy has assumed a capacity for distance, that is, to separate one's Self from that which is being studied or considered. Ontological awareness is an integration of the whole person with the whole experience.

The seeds of this type of awareness could be seen among the children described above. Their conscious, bodily and tactile encounter with the materials they were manipulating were experiences that appeared to engage their whole Selves, and so bridge the divide between Self and object, albeit for a short time. It seemed as if each child and the activity in which she or he was engaged had merged into a single entity. There was a connectedness – a unity – between the child and the activity. While they may not have been aware of the presence of others around them, these children were ontologically aware of themselves and their connectedness to the activity in which the divide between Self and object had been bridged.

The experiences of these children were holistic. They seemed to bridge the divides between Self and everything that was Other than Self. In these holistic experiences of unity, it was possible that these children were being led to a sense of their unity with Other in the more cosmic dimensions – in creation, and possibly in the Transcendent. At one level of consciousness, these children were physically present within close proximity to one another in a classroom space that had been provided for the conducting of this research. Yet, at another level, the children appeared to have removed themselves from this physical context of the classroom and from their peers into another dimension of being in which they were unified with their actions – one with Other. This accords with de Souza's (2004, 2006) notion of journeying towards Ultimate Unity, and with the concept of the unitary continuum (Newberg *et al.* 2001). It is more than likely that the children themselves would not have been able to articulate this experience since it was more primal than thought or language (Gendlin 1981). It was a tactile, sensorial and bodily experience of being – an experience of being whole. In this act of being, Merton might have said, these children had perhaps experienced something of the presence of God, for God had been present to them in the very act of their own being (Del Prete 2002). In other words, the unity experienced was possibly Ultimate Unity, in which the children had momentarily become one with Other.

Disintegration of space

In bridging such a divide, there was an interesting quality to the space that existed between each child and the activity to which she or he was attending. Perhaps it might be better envisaged as a closing of space, or even a disintegration of space. There was a sense in which the space that physically separated each child from her or his activity seemed to disintegrate as the conscious perception of bodily awareness led each child to an experience of unity with their activity. Such spaces of separation seemed to disappear as the whole Self of each child was engaged in the whole activity. This was particularly the case for Adam in Year 5 from the suburban school, and for Tran and Marco in Year 3 from the inner city school. For a short time, it literally seemed that there was no space between each of these children and their particular activity. The two had, as it were, become one. There was no divide between object and Self. These were holistic experiences in which Self became unified with that which was other than Self. In this experience of unity between Self and that which was other than Self, any notion of a space of separation ceased to exist.

A cocooned space

There were also two particular qualities to the space that existed *between* each of the children in the groups. The first of these spaces could best be described as a 'cocooned' space, particularly evident among the Year 5 children in the suburban school and the Year 3 children in the inner city school. In both these groups, the children, although seated in close proximity to one another, seemed oblivious to the presence of their peers. The physical distance that separated them was only a few feet, in some cases less. However, in these instances, the space seemed to act as a barrier. It was as if the children had created a 'cocooned' space that enabled them to focus their attention solely on their chosen activity. This space they created was important and necessary for their engagement in their chosen task, and could perhaps have been regarded as sacred space. It was respected, honoured and almost revered. None of the other children attempted to enter the space that surrounded any one particular child and her or his activity. This was a space of quiet. It was a space of tranquility in a room surrounded by the hustle and bustle of activity in a typical primary school. It was a space in which the felt sense could manifest itself, and in which the children could attend to their perception of bodily awareness in relation to the activity in which each was engaged.

A Collective Self

In some instances too, there was a second particular quality to the space that existed *between* each of the children in the group. Kristy and her friends involved in completing the jigsaw puzzle provide a good example of such a space. At its best, it can be described as a relational space. These children engaged in the tactile activity of completing the jigsaw collectively. This space, created by the children themselves, gave rise to a particular type of relationship that was experienced between each of the children in that group. It was a relationship of common purpose. They moved their arms and hands across each other's in the search for the correct pieces of the jigsaw. They talked with one another with their conversation focused on the task in which they were engaged. These children had become one with each other in their unified mission of completing the jigsaw. Each child, although distinct and inherently different from his or her peers, played a particular role in completing the jigsaw, and so became united *in* the task. Each used her or his individual talents and skills in the unified undertaking of the jigsaw puzzle. It could in fact be understood that each of these children had become one body with many parts to play in the successful completion of this task (cf. Corinthians 12:12–27) – the emergence of a Collective Self.

The notion of a Collective Self is pertinent. Its emergence seemed to entail a movement in which each individual Self became unified with every other Self among the group of children. Every Other – each other child with her or his Self – composed this Collective Self, in which Self had become one with Other. In this sense, a movement towards Ultimate Unity (de Souza 2004, 2006) may entail the emergence of a Collective Self, in which, at the deepest (inward) and widest (outward) levels of connectedness, Self and Other become one and the same.

The present moment of experience

In being absorbed in the activities in which they were engaged, each of the children was effectively attending to the here and now of their experience. The children seemed to be aware only of the present moment of their experience. For example, in completing the bead creation activity, Marco appeared to focus his attention immediately. His comment 'I'm going to finish this' may perhaps have suggested that, for him, time was not going to avert him from finishing the task. For Marco, time was literally going to stand still. His awareness was focused on what he was doing rather then the passing of time. The children in Year 5 from the rural school completing the jigsaw were also engaged in the present moment of their experience. They seemed not to have noticed the passing of time. When I announced that it was almost time to finish, there were cries of disappointment and surprise that a 30 minute passage of time could have passed so quickly. They had experienced the relativity of time. For them, time had somehow sped up in their enjoyment and engagement in the jigsaw activity, and they experienced the passing of time subjectively rather than objectively.

Donaldson (1992) referred to this immediacy of awareness as the *point mode*. As one of the most basic operations of the mind, point mode has prominence in children even after they have developed the capacity to focus on the past and future of experience. Another scholar, Trudelle Thomas (2001) refers to this same phenomenon as an immediate temporal horizon. Young children are adept at maintaining their focus in an immediate temporal horizon. It is something that they do quite naturally. It is, however, a skill that many adults seem to have lost. For as children develop, grow and become adults, engagement in point mode gradually gives way to *line mode* (Donaldson 1992), that is, the ability to focus on the past and future. While this is a necessary developmental process in the human person, it would appear that most adults have been conditioned to favour and engage in line mode. By the time children have reached adolescence, their ability to maintain a focus in the immediate temporal horizon has diminished considerably. In the business that typifies life in Western secular countries, many adults have all but lost the ability to engage in the immediacy of their awareness (see for example Hart 2003; Hay and Nye 2006; Thomas 2001). It is a skill that needs to be recovered and reclaimed.

Yet it would appear that an ability to engage in the here and now of time, the present moment of experience, is a necessary skill for spiritual development. It was in the immediate temporal horizon that the encounter between the children in my research and their activity became unified. It was in this particular experience of time that the divide between Self and object – the space of separation – ceased to exist, resulting in a unified apperception.

In a Nutshell

- The felt sense, as a characteristic of children's spirituality, seemed to entail the immediacy of experience – the here and now of time – and the individual drawing upon the wisdom of the body, as a natural way of knowing.

- This perception of bodily awareness, although more primal than thought or words, appeared to be a conscious, relational awareness on the part of these children. This may accord with Hay and Nye's (2006) notion of spirituality as relational consciousness – a conscious awareness of Self and everything Other than Self.

- In some instances, this sense of connectedness seemed to go beyond conventional notions of relationality, and could be described in terms of a unity between Self and everything Other than Self. Such a notion accords with the understanding and descriptions of spirituality I offered in Chapter 2, where spirituality may involve a movement towards Ultimate Unity. The children in my study appeared to have experienced something of this type of unity, albeit momentarily.

- In some instances, the felt sense also led to the emergence of a Collective Self, in which Self became unified with Other *in* the common task – every Other composed the Collective Self.

Some Guidelines for Nuturing the Felt Sense

In concluding this chapter, I wish to suggest some ways in which parents, teachers, and others who work with children may nurture the felt sense as a characteristic of children's spirituality.

- Allow children to engage with the sensory, ordinary and everyday activities of childhood. The kinds of tasks that led the children to experience the felt sense – completing jigsaw puzzles, planting seeds, painting or drawing, placing beads onto a stencil – comprised the ordinary, typical and everyday events of childhood. These types of activities, as well as others like running, skipping, swinging, singing, to name but a few, abound in the world of the child. Not all of them are necessarily spiritual, but when children engage in them, and draw upon their felt sense, many of these activities could be experienced as spiritual. The challenge for parents, teachers, and others who work with children is to recognize that these activities could possibly be experienced by children as spiritual. This is a difficult challenge, especially considering that Western culture has conditioned most adults to ignore their own felt sense. How can we recognize it in children?

- Allow children the time to engage in the present moment of their experience. In the secular Western world in which we live, this is difficult. The pace of life is fast and time to stop, or at least to slow down, is considered to be a commodity that cannot be afforded. Parents, where possible, try not to always be in a hurry. Slow the pace of life down a little, and allow your children time to play, to observe the tiny insects on the footpath, or the fog on a winter's day, or the leaves falling in autumn, and allow children simply the time to be. For teachers in the classroom, plan time into the curriculum for children to engage in the here and now, and, when the opportunity presents itself, be brave enough to make time for this, even if it means other planned tasks are left uncompleted – for a while at least.

- Include, within the curriculum, opportunities for children to manipulate and use tactile and sensory materials. It can be tempting for teachers to use work sheets or other tasks that involve only the processes of reading and writing. Try to diversify, and have the children discover and inquire for themselves through the use of materials that can be manipulated by them. In other words, allow them the opportunity to learn by drawing upon the wisdom of their bodies.

- For early years classrooms especially, build into the curriculum time for children to engage in play, both structured and unstructured. Play is the child's work. Through play, children may draw upon the wisdom of their bodies as a primal way of knowing. That is, they may draw upon their felt sense.

- For middle years classrooms within the primary school, make a conscious effort to build some form of play into the curriculum. This may assist children to maintain the skill of being able to engage in point mode – the present moment of experience – while their ability to engage in line mode develops.

- Encourage children to engage in group activity. This provides opportunities for children to interact relationally and possibly for a Collective Self to emerge.

- Consider carefully the types of spaces that are provided for children. Some spaces are toxic. They are filled with unnecessary business, with cynicism, and even competition. Other spaces encourage children to take risks, affirm children in their efforts, and encourage them to interact meaningfully with those around them.

- Be mindful of the spaces that exist *between* children in a group as well as the space connecting a child to her or his activity. Sometimes, children may require a 'cocooned', or sacred space in which to be alone to engage in activity. At other times, a more communal space may be necessary. The latter type of space may give rise to the notion of a Collective Self, in which children become unified in their joint undertaking of a task.

- Set aside time for yourself as an adult to engage in the here and now of your own experience. Again this is difficult. But if we are to nurture the spirituality of the children we parent, or with whom we work, then it is imperative that we tend to our own sense of being, and our own felt sense. How can we recognize the felt sense in our children if we do not acknowledge and recognize it within ourselves? There is a need to recover and reclaim the ability to know with our bodies, and to balance this with the intellectual way of knowing that is favoured by Western culture. Planning time for ourselves is an essential element in this process. Such time does not mean time spent in front of the television! Spend the time walking in the park or garden, or by being present to a friend in genuine conversation.

CHAPTER 6

Integrating Awareness

The characteristic of *integrating awareness* was observed particularly during the second phase of the awareness sensing meetings with the Year 5 children from the inner city school, the Year 3 children from the suburban school, and the Year 3 children from the rural school. Initially, it seemed to involve the typical elements of the flow experience (Csikszentmihalyi 1975). The children appeared to begin concentrating upon the activity they chose to undertake. After a short time, however, it was as if their chosen activity seemed to manage itself, thereby allowing the children to transcend the activity, and to enter into a 'free-flowing' style of conversation. At one level of awareness, their concentration remained on the activity at hand. Yet at a second level of awareness, they were able to speak freely and in an uninhibited manner, oblivious to the fact that I was present, and that they were being videotaped. Their conversation seemed to take on a life of its own, and it was the activity in which the children were engaged that seemed to enable this to happen. It was almost as if the activity enabled the children to transcend it, and to speak freely in conversation. Yet, as they spoke freely in conversation, the care which they displayed in attending to the activity did not diminish. The conversation seemed to have integrated with the activity. That is, this second level of awareness had enveloped or become integrated with the first level. In each case, after a time, one of the children became conscious of the presence of the adult and the video camera, and reminded her or his peers of this. At this point, a quiet resumed and the children's focus would return solely to the activity at hand.

The following reflective journal entry on the awareness sensing meeting with Year 5 children of the inner city school provides an example of integrating awareness. All of the children in this group had chosen the 'bead creations' activity, and after their concentration had become focused on the task at hand, a second level of awareness seemed to develop among them, manifest in the form of free-flowing conversation:

'When we're noisy, you're quiet, and when you're noisy, we're quiet,' began May Ling, who smiled as her comment was met with laughter.

'Like on camp,' interjected Hy Sun. 'Our cabin was so quiet, but Wadi couldn't stop snoring!'

'Me and Jack fell asleep straight away,' added Ramsay, 'but Albert kept on chanting "Aaaaanthony, Aaaaanthony".'

There was more laughing, followed by Fadde, who declared 'We were the noisiest cabin. Mr Marks and Miss Phoebe had to shout at us...'

'Those two love each other!' interrupted Missal, to the sound of further giggling.

'We had to get changed in our cabins,' continued Fadde, 'but every time Jack had to get changed he asked us to close our eyes...'

'And you should hear how he blows his nose!' added May Ling. 'It is so quiet, but when he blows his nose everyone went "ew!"'

'Oops – the camera is listening!' cautioned Hy Sun, who, while looking around, had suddenly become aware of the video and my presence.

Similarly, the following reflective journal entry on the Year 3 children from the suburban school provides some evidence of this characteristic of their spirituality. These children had all selected the seed planting activity, and after a short silence and time of focusing on the task, a second level of consciousness seemed to emerge among them, evident again through the particular style of conversation which developed. So free was their conversation that it was almost as if they had become oblivious to my presence and the video camera recording the meeting.

'Joseph gets to sleep in the lounge room,' declared Stacey.

'I get to sleep in the kitchen!' announced Joseph, who seemed pleased to be the centre of attention.

'No, Joseph sleeps with Sally!' exclaimed Milly.

'No, I don't!' retorted Joseph.

'As if!' replied a defiant Sally.

'Yes you do!' teased Milly.

'You're being silly,' giggled Sally.

Stacey turned towards the camera and said in a more serious tone, 'Is this (the video) going to be shown to our mums and dads?'

Trying my best to act impartially and not to react to the comments of their conversation, I assured them that the video would not be viewed by anyone other than myself.

'Good,' and 'That's OK then,' came their replies simultaneously.

Quiet descended upon the group as children's focus returned to the task at hand.

'Don't you dare tell my mum [that I said that],' cautioned Milly in a quiet voice to Emma. 'She's going to kill me!'

The Year 3 children from the rural school setting provided a variation on this characteristic of integrating awareness. While this group did engage in conversation, their conversation seemed to be largely task oriented. There was a communal purpose to their engagement in their activity, as the following reflection indicates:

> The children divided themselves into three smaller groups to work on different sections of the jigsaw. There was a sense of cooperation, but more than this. There was a sense of relationality. It occurred to me that this jigsaw activity was being completed in relationship with Other. There was a sense of group spirit. All group members were needed, and had an important role to play in completing the task. Various pieces of the jigsaw were passed from group to group, according to the sections that were being worked upon. There was a sense of purpose and engagement in this activity. In this instance, the activity took care of itself, but only in relation to the Other. As the activity proceeded, some conversation was generated, but mostly in relation to the task at hand, and for the most part, it was undertaken in quiet whispers.

Integrating awareness, as a characteristic of children's spirituality, seemed to entail the emergence of a second wave of consciousness, typified by a free-flowing style of conversation, which enveloped, or became integrated at an initial level of consciousness, which featured an attention to tactile, hands-on activity.

A Reflection and Discussion on Integrating Awareness

The interesting thing to note with integrating awareness is that, when it became evident, the children were all engaged in the same initial activity, whether it was seed planting, 'bead creations', completing a jigsaw, or drawing and painting. In these instances, it seemed that the children wished to enter the interpersonal space shared by the group through conversation, while at the same time the very activity which the group chose to complete provided an initial foundation for their conversation.

Primarily, integrating awareness seemed to involve the children in experiences of flow (Csikszentmihalyi 1975). They appeared to be concentrating upon the activity in which each was engaged, attending to the here and now of experience. However, as the children began to master the skills needed to complete their task, they appeared to reach another level of consciousness whereby they were able enter into a particular style of 'free-flowing' conversation with those around them. At one level of awareness, their concentration remained on the activity in which they were engaged. Yet at a second level, they were able to speak freely with each other in an uninhibited way. Their conversation seemed to take on a life of its own, and the activity in which they were engaged seemed to enable this to happen. This could be seen in the fact that their absorption in the activity at the initial level of awareness did not simply become a mechanical response. The care with which the children attended to their tasks continued even as they began to engage in this second level of awareness. This may be a feature of situations in which children are absorbed in 'hands-on' type activities, such as those involving art or craft. The physical action of the children in attending to these types of activities at this level of awareness may prepare the ground for another level of awareness to emerge.

While the work of Csikszentmihalyi (1975, 1990), Gendlin (1962, 1981) and Hay and Nye (2006) in part explains the concentrated awareness, there appeared to be something else occurring here. The conversation in which the children were engaged seemed to have assimilated the activity. Put another way, a second level of consciousness had encased, or become integrated with the first level. This accords with the traditional Eastern notions of interconnecting levels of consciousness as presented by Aurobindo (Marshak and Litfin 2002), and Fontana (2003), and by Wilber (2000b), who made a sustained attempt to link such developmental levels of consciousness with Western science. This was discussed in Chapter 2. Integrating awareness is the phrase I have used to describe this particular characteristic, in which an emerging level of consciousness appeared to have become integrated with an existing level of awareness.

While acknowledging the complexity and uncertainty in discussing the nature of consciousness, the work of transpersonal psychologist Ken Wilber provides a helpful model for exploring the characteristic termed integrating awareness.

The integrating function of Self

In discussing the different waves, lines and states that might comprise an integral theory of consciousness, Wilber (2000a, b) argued that there are various developmental levels of awareness that unfold in a person. They are termed developmental not because they are rigid or linear, but because they are fluid, and overlap, similar to the way in which waves by the seaside appear to overlap and enfold each other. Wilber applied this idea to describe the developmental unfolding of consciousness. The higher levels of consciousness do not sit on top of the lower dimensions like rungs in a ladder, but rather they enfold them, just as, for example, cells embody molecules which embody atoms. These developmental waves appear to be like 'concentric spheres of increasing embrace, inclusion, and holistic capacity' (Wilber 2000a, p.147).

Central to this is the notion of the Self, or Self system, which acts as a means by which to integrate, or balance these waves of consciousness.[13] Wilber maintained that waves of consciousness, as well as other aspects of awareness, appear to be devoid of an intrinsic self-sense. One of the primary characteristics of Self is its capacity to identify with basic waves of consciousness, and to integrate the various components of the psyche. In psychopathology, for instance, the basic waves of consciousness would be considered to emerge in a generally well-functioning manner. The basic structures of consciousness do not in themselves become 'broken'. When, for example, concrete operational thinking emerges in a child, it does so more or less intact. However, what the child does with that wave of consciousness specifically involves the child's sense of Self and the ability of the Self system to *integrate* the emerging wave of consciousness with previous waves. It is possible, according to Wilber, that a child may take any of the tenants of the concrete operational mind and repress them, alienate them, project them, or effectually deploy any number of other defensive mechanisms. This represents an illness, not of concrete operational thinking, but of the Self.

This process of integration occurs each time Self encounters a new wave of consciousness. According to Wilber, the Self system must firstly identify, or be in fusion with that new wave. Secondly, Self must *disidentify*, or transcend that level so as to move to a yet higher wave. Then, ideally, Self integrates the previous wave of consciousness with the higher wave. Fusion, transcendence, and integration occur each time the Self system encounters a new wave of consciousness.

Wilber's model serves to inform the characteristic I have termed integrating awareness. In each case, an initial level of consciousness was encountered by each child's Self system. This comprised the activity in which they were engaged. Their focus, concentration and absorption in this corporeal activity may have indicated that Self had already integrated this level with previous waves of consciousness. Then, the Self systems of these children encountered a new level of consciousness – the particular type of conversation that was emerging among them. The children seemed to gravitate towards this new level, each child making a contribution to the ebb and flow of the conversation. In other words, Self fused with this emerging level. Self then transcended this level so as to integrate this new wave of consciousness with the previous. The result of this integration of consciousness by Self was that the new level of consciousness – the free-flowing conversation – enveloped or integrated the previous level of engagement with the activity. Evidence of this integration could be seen in the fact that the task being undertaken by the children continued to be completed with care and skill. There was a quality to their work that suggested their completion of the task was not simply a mechanical response. Rather, the conversation – the new level of consciousness – had integrated the activity.

A relational space

There was also a sense in which the children collectively seemed to have created a particular type of space in which to accommodate the emerging level of consciousness. It had been prepared by the children in choosing to undertake the same tactile and sensorial task. The commonality of the task then seemed to provide an impetus for conversation. Although there was initially very little talking, as children mastered the skills needed to complete the task, conversation began to emerge. In other words, in attending initially to their activity, the ground was prepared through the creation of an appropriate space, for the emerging level of awareness. While this space could be described as one of invitation, since all children contributed to the ebb and flow of the conversation, it was also a confidential space. It needed to be if the particular type of conversation that emerged – itself somewhat inappropriate for the supervised classroom context – was to develop freely and without hindrance in a space in which both the context and content of the discourse was respected. The children seemed to sense this, and, while often oblivious to my presence and to my videotaping them, they sought to remind me of the confidentiality of the space they had created. Hy Sun's comment 'Oops – the camera is listening' was as much a reminder to me as to his peers of the protected space that had been created. Stacey's question, 'Is this (the video) going to be shown to our mums and dads?' was almost certainly a request for me, as the researcher, to honour the space that had been established. It was in this space that these children were exhibiting a characteristic of their spirituality, namely the ability to integrate an emerging wave of consciousness with a previous level of awareness.

Further, this space enabled the children to become less self conscious and to connect with Other through conversation. Therefore, this space could also be described as *relational*. Each of the children who were physically present within that particular space was able to relate through conversation with their peers. All contributions to the conversation were welcomed. No one was excluded. In other words, each of the children contributed to the whole, and were connected in relationship through means of the conversation. Integrating awareness seemed to demand such a space in which the emerging wave of consciousness could develop among the children freely.

Merging of temporal horizons

The children seemed, at the same time, to be both aware of attending to the activity and conscious of their conversation with their peers. In other words, their awareness was focused on the present moment of their experience. In this present moment the children experienced a merging of temporal horizons – immediate past, present and the immediate future. The immediate past temporal horizon consisted of their engagement in their chosen activity. It included their focus, their concentration and mastery of the skills necessary to complete the particular task. Yet, this horizon seemed to merge with the present temporal horizon, in which the activity continued to be undertaken while a particular free-flowing style of conversation developed among them. In this present or immediate temporal horizon the characteristic of integrating awareness was exhibited. The children were unified with the task they had begun in the immediate past *and* with the conversation that was emerging in the present. It seemed also that all of this merged with the immediate future temporal horizon as the children anticipated the direction of the conversation and contributed to its ebb and flow. The children did not seem to control the conversation, as this took on a life of its own and dictated its own direction. As is the case with all genuine conversations, the children found themselves to be less leaders of it than they were led by it (cf. Gadamer 1989). Yet, each child, in risking and offering her or his own contribution to the conversation anticipated its possible course, like players in a game attempting to predict their opponent's next move. The outcome of the conversation, like that of a game, was unknown. But the various possibilities, the potential twists and turns, the likely plays with and plays upon words were sought in advance by the children involved. In this way the immediate future merged with the present and immediate past temporal horizons. Situated in this temporal sequence, the children perhaps experienced the passing of time as a unified and simultaneous flowing from one moment to the next (cf. Merleau-Ponty 1996) – from the immediate past, through the present to the immediate future. Yet at any one moment in time, all three temporal horizons could have been understood to coexist, that is, to have merged into a single temporal horizon. There was a sense in which any one particular moment in time could have been understood to contain the immediate past, present and immediate future as a single entity.

Corporeal foundations

The corporeal and tactile activities in which the children were engaged could be understood to provide a foundation for this emerging wave of consciousness. The conscious perception of physical bodily awareness – the felt sense of these children seemed to act in such a way as to prepare the ground for the emerging wave of consciousness to develop and integrate the previous level. In each case, it was only after the children's engagement in the initial sensorial tasks that the particular style of conversation began to emerge. Without the children's engagement in these activities, it is possible that the characteristic of integrating awareness may not have become evident. Physical and bodily engagement by the children was then a necessary prerequisite in preparing the ground for the emergence of this new wave of consciousness and its integration with previous levels.

Perhaps these two waves of consciousness were interdependent. The physical and tactile experiences were needed in order to provide a foundation for the emerging wave of consciousness. Yet this new level of awareness was itself needed so that integrating awareness could occur. In a sense, consciousness generated other levels of consciousness. Neither wave was more important or more integral than the other. Both were required for Self to move through the phases of fusion, transcendence and integration. Both were then necessary for the children's expression of the spiritual characteristic of integrating awareness.

In a Nutshell

- Integrating awareness seemed to entail the emergence of a new or second wave of consciousness, typified in my study by a free-flowing style of conversation, which enveloped, or integrated an initial level of awareness which featured an attention to tactile, hands-on activity.

- The initial corporeal, sensorial activities in which the children engaged seemed to provide a foundation – to prepare the ground for the emerging level of consciousness.

- Integrating awareness was evident in a space that could be described as safe, confidential, relational and invitational.

- Integrating awareness encompassed three temporal dimensions – immediate past, present and immediate future.

- Self's drive to integrate an emerging wave of consciousness with a previous level through fusion, transcendence and integration, in order to relate to Other at the very least suggests that integrating awareness could be a characteristic of spirituality.

Throughout history, there have been individuals from various religious traditions who appear to have been able to do precisely this – to integrate a new emerging level of consciousness in order to enter into relationship with the Transcendent. Those who have been able to do this at sophisticated levels could include the prophet Mohammed and Sufi master Ibn Al-'Arabi. In the Christian tradition, it could be argued that Jesus himself was able to do this in discerning his identity and relationship with God, who he called Father. The Christian mystics such as St Teresa of Jesus and St John of the Cross were also able to integrate awareness in attaining higher levels of consciousness in order to enter into relationship with the divine ground of their being – God.

To detail one brief example, in *The Interior Castle*, St Teresa of Jesus (1577) wrote of the dignity of the human being as the dwelling place of God. In attaining a higher level of consciousness and integrating it with previous levels, she spoke of the soul as being the interior castle, the place where God resides, and of prayer as being the means by which the soul is united to God. Through prayer St Teresa wrote of a higher consciousness that the individual can attain by which she or he may reach the boundaries of this ultimate relationship, or union. In other words, St Teresa of Jesus was able to integrate higher levels of consciousness with previous levels through which to experience union with God.

My study indicates the possibility that children of primary school age are able to do this at more basic and less sophisticated levels. The fact that children are able to integrate new waves of consciousness with their previous levels of awareness suggests that integrating awareness is at least a characteristic of Self's drive to integrate, and therefore, it could possibly be identified as a characteristic of their spirituality.

Some Guidelines for Nurturing Integrating Awareness

Integrating awareness is the ability to integrate new emerging waves of consciousness with previous levels of awareness. While it is a phenomenon that has been accomplished by the mystics and sages of many faith traditions in order to achieve a state of unity with the divine, my study has suggested that children are capable of integrating awareness too, albeit at less sophisticated and more basic levels.

However, a key to the emergence of this particular characteristic is the preparing of the ground in terms of the initial tactile and sensory experiences which are provided. Even in the case of, let us say, a Buddhist monk who is an accomplished meditator, and who integrates an emerging wave of consciousness – the state of *anatta* – with an awareness of the present moment of experience, tactile and sensory activity is initially involved. Invariably, this takes the form of focusing on the rhythm of breathing, or becoming aware of the sensation of the physical body upon the hard surface of the floor. In the Christian tradition, manipulation of beads, such a rosary beads, or concentrating one's visual focus on an object such as a candle or crucifix, may prepare the ground for an emerging wave of consciousness to integrate with a previous level of awareness.

Below are some suggestions for how integrating awareness might be nurtured in children.

- Prepare the ground. As parents, teachers, and others who work with children, it may be that, through a child's carefully set up bedroom or play area, or through a prepared classroom environment, we have in fact prepared a conducive space with possible sensory activity with which the child might engage to enable integrating awareness to occur. I am not suggesting that children regularly integrate higher levels of consciousness, or attain deep meditative states. However, and as my own research indicates, given that children show a capacity to integrate emerging levels of consciousness with previous levels of awareness, are we as adults (parents, teachers, kindergarten directors, and the like) aware of this capacity of children, and are we prepared to provide an environment in which children have the opportunity to develop their spirituality in this particular way?

- Attention to the types of spaces that are created in kindergartens and classrooms, and allowing children to create their own spaces in which to express and nurture their spirituality is pertinent. In some instances, and as evidenced earlier in this chapter, if such spaces are to be characterized by safety and confidentiality, teachers may need to be willing to remove themselves from the spaces that children create in order for children to nurture their own spirituality. I am not suggesting that teachers need to leave their classrooms or learning areas, but rather that, when necessary, they give children a space which will not be intruded upon by themselves as the adult authority figure. This is challenging, and may require some educators to rethink their provision of space, or even to undertake further professional development in this area.

- Teachers in faith schools are well placed to provide opportunities for integrating awareness to occur, particularly through the use of sensorial materials as a component in the religious education curriculum. Such materials could be used as a vehicle to prayer. For instance, in exploring the theme of creation, enabling the children to engage initially in an activity such as modelling with clay, and then being invited to name silently to God those attributes, skills or talents that make them unique, may enable integrating awareness to occur. In Sunday School settings, particularly those modelled on the Godly Play (Berryman 1991) approach, or the Catechesis of the Good Shepherd (Cavalletti 1983), the use of sensorial materials, which are key to both approaches, may provide opportunities for integrating awareness to occur.

- As parents, teachers, and others who work with children, provide some opportunities for silence and solitude, so that children can become aware of, for example, the rhythm of their breathing, their bodies upon the surface of the floor. This need not be an ardent attempt at meditation (although for some it could), but rather gently providing time for children to develop those skills that are required for quiet and contemplation. These may lead to opportunities for integrating awareness.

- Where appropriate, particularly at home, or possibly even within the classroom, provide opportunities for guided meditation. Jenny Garth's books *Starbright* (1992) and *Earthlight* (1997) provide excellent guided meditations for young children, and are intended for use particularly at home, but can be drawn upon in the classroom. The particular guided meditations devised by Garth do not have a religious focus, and so can be drawn upon comfortably in a variety of settings, both secular and religious.

CHAPTER 7

Weaving the Threads
of Meaning

The second group meeting with children in my research focused on the concept of mystery sensing (Hay and Nye 2006). Mystery sensing involves the sense of wonder and awe, the fascination and questioning which is characteristic of children as they interact with the mystery of the universe. The second phase of this group meeting entailed the children's reactions and points of discussion in relation to a series of photographs which I had shown to them. It was hoped that these photographs might generate some reflective conversation around the notions of mystery and wonder.

In each of the mystery sensing group meetings, it became clear that the children's sense of wonder acted as a tool for expressing their spirituality. The children seemed to draw upon their sense of wonder in order to make meaning of events and to piece together a worldview based around their attempts at meaning-making. Since the act of meaning-making is continuous and ongoing, the children's own creating of their spirituality was also a work in progress. It is interesting to note that this active creating seems to have occurred despite the fact that these children were immersed in school contexts that presented and promoted the Catholic faith tradition, and hence a Catholic worldview. These children did not draw solely from the Christian meta-narrative in creating and expressing their spirituality. Rather, they seemed to draw upon an eclectic range of concepts and ideas to develop a personal framework that enabled them to make meaningful connections with the Transcendent and with others. In terms of Western culture, Horell (2004) has expressed such a notion in terms of a shift away from a focus on adherence to a Christian religious worldview towards a greater emphasis on the importance of spiritual experiences, and the notion of connecting spiritually with Self, others, the world, and with God. Such a shift seemed to be evident in these children, who were effectively able to weave together strands of meaning from their pluralistic, multicultural world into a framework that provided 'a sense of personal centeredness and enable[d] them to make meaningful connections with God and others' (p.8). In drawing upon Horell's notion, the characteristic expressed by the children in this present study has been termed *weaving the threads of meaning.*

The children's reactions and conversation generated in relation to three of the photographs shown to them were particularly indicative of their ability to utilize their sense of wonder in order to weave together the threads of meaning. The first of these three pictures was a large panoramic photograph of Uluru, a large rock formation in Central Australia. The following reflective journal entry on the Year 3 children in the inner city school exemplifies this characteristic:

> The children's faces displayed expressions of amazement as I showed them the panoramic photograph of Uluru...
>
> 'I wonder: how did it get so big?' (asked Rosie)
>
> 'I wonder if it is a volcano,' said Ali, who seemed to be drawing upon some recent work in the classroom which had involved an exploration of a volcano that had erupted some time ago.
>
> 'No,' interjected Rosie, 'it's just a rock.'
>
> 'But how did it get there?' wondered Charlotte. There was something about this particular photograph that seemed to have captured her attention.
>
> 'Well, maybe it just dropped from the sky,' offered Tran.
>
> 'Yes, but it's huge!' exclaimed Charlotte.
>
> 'It could have fallen, like how hail stones come out of the sky,' replied Rosie, 'and there could have been so many of them, and the Aboriginals [sic] could have stacked them up and painted the rock that red colour.'
>
> 'But the hail would have melted,' said Charlotte, who seemed a little disappointed that Rosie's theory could be flawed so easily.
>
> 'Maybe a volcano somewhere erupted,' said Ali, attempting to take up and build upon Rosie's theme with his own creation, 'and all the rocks came and landed there. A few days later, they somehow got stacked together.'
>
> 'Well,' began Rosie, 'maybe it could have been part of a volcano that disappeared, and it just came to be rocks and it was all mushy and some people pushed it up and made it tall and it went hard.'
>
> 'The lava might have made it that colour,' added Tran, who was eager not to be left out of the conversation.

Similarly, the following reflective journal entry on the Year 3 students in the suburban school illustrates the ability to draw upon wonder as a tool for weaving the threads of meaning. In this instance, the notion of God as creator was introduced into the discussion.

> 'Wow!'
>
> Such was the unanimous comment when I showed the children the large panoramic photograph of Uluru.
>
> 'Maybe there was once an ocean there, and when the waves came up and splashed against it, it carved the shape,' said Zephania.
>
> 'I think it was a volcano,' said Joseph, 'and when it erupted, the lava came down the side, and that's how it got its curves.'
>
> 'Maybe the marks [curves] were put there by the claws of a big animal, like maybe a dinosaur!' exclaimed Milly.
>
> 'Yes,' replied Joseph, 'I think it has been there since dinosaurs were alive.'
>
> 'Maybe God made it,' offered Sally.
>
> I took the opportunity of asking Sally what she meant by God. She confidently replied, 'God is our Father.'

The Year 5 children in the inner city school found this meeting difficult. Their body language seemed to suggest that they were disinterested and even mistrustful of each other and their responses. Their flippant and off-hand remarks, as well as their constant giggling indicated that they had created a façade of facetiousness which seemed to protect their safety zone. However, their reaction to the photograph of Uluru was an instance in which these children displayed some insight into their genuine wondering, and their ability to draw upon it as a means by which to weave together the different strands of meaning:

> When I showed the panoramic photograph of Uluru, their body language changed. They edged forward for a closer look, saying, 'It's Uluru, it's Uluru!'
>
> 'How did it get like that?' wondered Missal, almost oblivious to the fact that she had broken her façade.
>
> 'It's in the middle of nowhere,' added Hy Sun, who had become momentarily mesmerized by the photograph. His eyes were opened wide and his mouth was ajar.
>
> 'Maybe God created it,' began Maria, 'and it slowly began to grow bigger and bigger...'
>
> 'Maybe there are spirits there,' said Missal, 'and people distract them...'
>
> 'By walking all over it,' interjected Maria, 'and the spirits get angry.'

'It might have been a volcano,' suggested Ramsey, 'that was slowly shrinking.'

'And it's got that funny red colour,' added May Ling, 'maybe because of the sun. It's hot in the Northern Territory.'

'Maybe the Aborigines painted it,' commented Missal to the sounds of relieved laughter. The safety zone had been restored and the children could again return to familiar territory.

The second of the three photographs that provided the impetus for drawing upon their ability to utilize their sense of wonder in order to create meaning, was the photograph of two young children crying. In many cases, children in each group wondered if the children in the photograph were crying because someone had died. This generated much discussion and attempts to fashion a particular meaning-making framework indicative of their spirituality, as can be seen in the following reflective journal entry on the Year 5 children in the suburban school.

'They look like someone might have died,' replied Adam. The rest of the group nodded in agreement.

'I wonder what you might say to make them feel better,' I probed.

'I'd say "Don't worry, they'll still be with you in your heart."'

'And that you'll always remember them,' added Alicia.

'And I'd tell them that they still have each other,' stated Adam.

There was a pause in the conversation, so I probed a little further. 'I wonder where the person who had died might have gone.'

'Their body would still be on earth, because it would have been buried,' said Alicia thoughtfully, 'but the soul would go to heaven.'

As the term 'heaven' had been introduced by the children themselves, I decided to explore this further with them:

'Well, heaven,' began Cameron, '…it's not like you can drive there. It's a thought; it's in your heart if you believe that it's there.'

'It's like a secret place,' explained Danny. 'No one has been there except for those who have died. No one knows where it is.'

'Heaven is…' [continued] John, who was struggling to find the right words to give expression to this thought, '…you can't really imagine it. We go there in our golden years, like, after we turn 50.'

One of the children then added that Jesus had told people about heaven, and although I wanted to explore this idea further, the conversation was quite suddenly taken by the children in a different direction:

'I actually think that everyone who has passed away…' began Danny, 'well, they have a different heaven. If a person liked painting, then they'd go to a place where you can paint all you want.'

'I'm reading a book,' added Alicia, 'about a girl who is thirteen years old and she dies and goes to this angel academy school in heaven. Once I had read that, I thought, that's where people go. They go into separate groups and do what they want to do and what they like to do.'

The Year 3 counterparts of these children in the suburban school similarly drew upon their sense of wonder in order to create a sense of meaning in relation to this photograph.

'Maybe someone died in their family,' offered Stacey.

'I wonder what you might say to the children to make them feel better,' I probed.

Joseph was the first to reply. 'I'd say, "Don't worry. If they've died, they're all around you."'

'I'd say that we'll all be up there one day,' added Emma. 'Everyone will go up to heaven and we'll stay there.'

I asked the children what it was that they meant by the word 'heaven'. 'It's where God is,' replied Joseph.

'It's a cloud, and a place where there is peace, and it's all white,' added Stacey.

'It's where nice people go when they die,' said Sally.

'I think heaven is maybe a happy place with waterfalls and rainforests,' suggested Milly.

'Heaven is like a new world,' declared Zephania.

'It's a place where God and Mary and Jesus live,' added Stacey.

The children in Year 5 in the inner city school were shown a third, slightly different photograph of an elderly lady, perhaps someone's grandmother. Although at times cautious and hesitant in their conversation, these children expressed something of their ability to weave together the threads of meaning when shown this photograph. After agreeing that the lady had died, I asked what the children might say to comfort her relatives:

'You'll still have memories of her,' said Maria.

'She's with you in spirit,' added May Ling. 'Just because she's not in front of you doesn't mean she's gone.'

'She's in your heart,' added Missal.

'If she was good,' began Hy Sun, 'she might be in heaven.'

I inquired as to what he meant by the word 'heaven'.

The responses came quickly – 'It's a good, peaceful place,' 'where God lives.' 'It's where good spirits go.'

'If she was not a good person on earth,' explained Hy Sun, 'she would remain a ghost and haunt people and their houses.'

'Yeah,' agreed Fadde, 'evil stuff would happen.'

'Or,' suggested Maria, 'she'd go to hell. It's a place of torture with the devil and his pitchfork.'

Similarly, the Year 3 children in the inner city school believed the lady in the photograph had died, and they set about weaving the threads of meaning.

'Maybe it's a photo of a lady who passed away,' said Marco, 'and they had a funeral for her with a photo like that one...'

'She might have got cremated,' added Rosie. 'They put you in a coffin and put it on fire, and then there's only ashes left and they put them in a jar and you keep it. Or, sometimes you can tip the ashes out in a spot that she liked.'

There followed a short pause, and then Charlotte said, 'Maybe she got buried and then her soul flew up to heaven.' As she said this, Charlotte placed her hands in the position of wings and fluttered them upwards. Then she quickly added, 'Or down to hell or to purgatory.'

'That's in between,' clarified Amina.

'Well, its exactly the same as hell, except one day you go to heaven,' replied Charlotte.

'And if you've been really bad, you go to hell,' said Rosie, eager to clarify further.

At this point, I asked the children what they meant by the term 'heaven'.

'Like, say if you're Catholic,' began Charlotte, 'heaven is a really happy place.'

'How would they make heaven happy and hell bad?' asked Tran, who seemed to now be wondering quite seriously about this.

'Do you know what purgatory means?' Rosie asked Charlotte. 'It's hard to explain.'

'I know how to explain it,' declared Charlotte confidently. 'My dad taught me because his mum is really Catholic. She has all these statues, and every day she says the rosary. She loves God. She used to go to church every day, but now she's too old. She only goes once a week.'

In a similar way, the conversation of the Year 3 children in the rural school focused around the idea of death when discussing the photograph of the elderly lady, and attempts were made to create meaning around this concept.

'She has probably died,' said Michael, 'and she was probably very special to her family because they wouldn't have bothered to put her photo in that pretty frame if she wasn't important to them.'

'She goes into a grave,' added Susan, 'and she'll go up to heaven.'

'Her soul goes up to heaven,' clarified Imelda.

'It's only our soul that goes up to heaven...depending on how good you are,' enlightened Tom.

I inquired what the children meant by the word 'heaven'.

'Paradise,' offered Michael after a moment's reflection. 'Heaven is paradise because people say they're in heaven when they are at a good place, or when they're doing something they really enjoy.'

'It's a peaceful, loving place,' added Imelda.

'She'll [the lady in the photograph] stay there for eternity.'

The notion of 'hell' was also raised during this discussion, and as the children appeared to be interested in this concept, I explored this term with them.

'It's a kind of death after death,' reflected Michael.

'It's a ball of fire,' explained Tom. 'Heaven is ruled by Jesus and God, but hell is ruled by the Devil, and the Devil is actually an angel that turned on God. Where there's heaven, there's probably hell too.'

'Everyone has a good side and a bad side,' explained Michael. 'It's like the good side says "Don't listen to him, he's the Devil", but the bad side says "Go on, flush your brother's mouth guard down the toilet!"'

The Year 5 children in the rural school spoke quite freely about the notion of death and afterlife without the need of a stimulus photograph. Some of these children indicated that these were concepts about which they frequently wondered. This may perhaps have been because many of these children's families came from farms, and they had seen first-hand the life cycles of the natural world. Such experiences may have allowed these children to be more comfortable with the topic of death and afterlife. The discussion that ensued in this particular group meeting flowed quite freely in an attempt to actively create meaning. The following reflection is indicative of this:

'I wonder about why people die and go up to heaven,' said Kristy. 'I wonder about what they do up in heaven, because, you see shows on TV where people in heaven play games, or can dance – if they were dancers when they were alive.'

'I wonder why some people die at 30 years,' said Emily, 'and why other people die at 100 years. I wonder why people who die at 30 don't live until 100. One of my uncles died at 27, but my grandpa died at 98. I wish that I had known him better when he was alive.'

'I wonder about why my sister died,' added Michelle, clasping her hands around herself, 'and if there was a reason – I can't really explain why. She pretty much died instantly, and I wonder why our family got someone who died.'

The researcher inquired what the children understood by the word 'heaven', which had been introduced into the conversation.

'It's hard to explain,' began Lara. 'It's like a second world.'

'No one on earth has seen it until they die,' added Michelle.

'One of my mum's uncles, he's been to heaven and come back,' remarked Annabelle, who had been quiet, and almost disinterested until now. The other children immediately turn to look at her with great interest. 'Well, he thinks he has seen it, because he's been in hospital a couple of times, and he's been in a coma. He woke up recalling hearing music and seeing all his [dead] relatives again.'

'My great nana is in an old folks' home,' explained Kristy, 'She had to be taken to hospital. During the night she wouldn't wake up, and she reckons she's seen heaven as well.'

'Sometimes we used to go to Port Fairy with my sister Kim before she died,' began Michelle, 'and one time when we went back there after she died, I thought I'd saw her walking behind me.'

This immediately captured the attention of the other children. One or two of them, who had been fidgeting, now look directly at Michelle for further details. Michelle seems to sense this, and although happy to reveal further, clasped her arms around her own body, as somehow indicating that this was *her* story. Her story was (and is) sacred, and although willing to share it with her peers, she was not ready to let go of it just yet.

'I was amazed,' continued Michelle 'that I actually saw her again because I was young and I thought I wouldn't see her again until I was really old and had died.'

Michelle was convinced that she had seen, or at the very least experienced her sister in this event in a profound way. So I asked if she remembered what Kim might have been wearing, or what she might have looked like.

'I think she had a pink dress on,' replied Michelle, 'but she was like a faded cloud, sort of – she didn't look alive – it was like a spirit sort of – I was walking behind Tom and Mum, and Kim was behind me.'

A Reflection and Discussion on Weaving the Threads of Meaning

The characteristic I have termed as weaving the threads of meaning suggests that the children were able to draw upon their inner qualities, particularly their sense of wonder in order to make meaning of events and to piece together a worldview based around their attempts at meaning-making. What was particularly interesting was that even though these children were immersed in contexts that promoted a Catholic worldview, they nonetheless seemed to draw upon an eclectic range of concepts and ideas to develop a personal framework that enabled them to make meaningful connections with others, and in some instances, with a Transcendent dimension. The Christian narrative was but one of many frameworks of meaning drawn upon by these children. And, they were totally unapologetic for its infrequent influence, preferring instead to draw from whatever frameworks provided significance for them.

Australian researcher Philip Hughes maintains that young people pick and choose from a range of frameworks in order to form their beliefs. In discussing this phenomenon, Hughes (2007) uses the term 'whateverism' to describe this picking and choosing. However, his use of the term 'whateverism' tends to suggest that this selecting by young people occurs in a somewhat random or arbitrary kind of manner. It is not so much of a searching among frameworks for genuine meaning, but rather an attitude of 'this will do' or as Hughes himself says 'Whatever floats your boat'. I would like to suggest that this piecing together of a worldview, at least among the children in my own research, appeared to be a much more deliberate act. There was a sense of intentionality about the way they pieced their worldview together. It was subjective, certainly, but not arbitrary.

Entering the space between the frameworks of meaning

The various frameworks which seemed to be drawn upon by the children in my own study included the media, their own experience, their prior learning, mythology, other faith traditions, as well as the Christian story, some parts of which, as the above texts show, were innovative. As I began to interpret the texts of my study, questions arose in relation to how these children then actually chose from among these different frameworks of meaning those aspects which offered personal significance for them. What was it, for example, that led them to draw from the media as opposed to the Christian tradition? Or, when they did draw upon the Christian narrative, what was it that led these children to innovate upon it, and choose selectively from within it? Upon reflection, it seemed that the children had in fact entered the space between each of these different frameworks in order to select eclectically those elements which created meaning for themselves. They were then able to weave together these threads of meaning into a personal framework which afforded them personal significance.

Webster's (2004) notion of an existential framework of spirituality is helpful here in shedding some light upon this characteristic of weaving the threads of meaning. Human beings are both historically and culturally embedded in terms of the particularities of the time and space in history in which they are situated. As such, people attempt to make sense of the world in which they find themselves from an already existing horizon of understanding. This horizon consists of the meanings received from the individual's social and cultural world that provide a code for how one might conduct one's life in order to satisfy, or comply with that which is expected as the norm in that culture.

However, existential philosophy would contend that while an individual is influenced by the historical, social and cultural elements that comprise this horizon of meaning, a person is not totally determined by them. A person is able to exercise a degree of agency that facilitates the formation of personal views and commitments (Webster 2004). In other words, the individual has choice.

The individual, as free to choose, is important. There exists a freedom that one can exercise in relation to the meanings that are received from her or his particular culture. Webster argues that there is a particular type of space that is created between the various frameworks of meaning that are offered by a culture or society, and the individually created meanings that offer personal significance for the individual. Such a space can create a tension between the meanings acquired from one's personal life experience, and what Chater (2001) refers to as received and authoritative wisdom of the culture, society, or presented worldview. It is Webster's contention that a person's spirituality emerges in this space as the result of the encounter between personal meaning and the frameworks provided by society. Spiritual development in fact requires the struggle of a person who strives to exercise a sense of freedom, deciding which meanings offer personal significance, and how she or he will relate to these.

Now, this idea can be applied to the findings of my research. If Christianity, as the overarching framework of the context in which these children were situated (the Catholic school) is considered to be the received and authoritative wisdom, it would seem that these children were exercising their personal sense of freedom. In other words, these children had entered the space between the different frameworks of meaning so as to exercise their freedom in choosing from among those the elements which offered some significance for them.

When, for example, the children were shown the panoramic photograph of Uluru, they drew upon many frameworks of meaning. In stating that this rock formation could once have been a volcano, as Joseph and Ali did, the children were drawing upon their prior learning experiences in the field of science. When Missal and Maria spoke about the spirits that might dwell on Uluru, it is possible that they were referring to the spirits of the indigenous people's ancestors who once lived there. Ramsey alluded to the Australian Aboriginal Dreamtime stories, while Sally drew upon the Judeo-Christian story in commenting that God had created it. In their wondering, these children seemed to have entered the space between the various frameworks of meaning, and exercised their freedom in selecting from those frameworks elements which were significant for them.

The media was a particularly influential framework. Its influence came to the fore when the children's discussion led to the notion of heaven and an afterlife. Kristy commented that on television, heaven is depicted as a place where people play games, or dance. Cameron had said heaven was in your heart if you believe it to be there. Danny maintained that heaven was different for every person, so that if someone liked to paint, then heaven would be a place where you can paint until your heart's content. Alicia likened heaven to an 'angel academy'. One common source for such ideas is the media, in its many forms – television, popular music, short novels, and the like. Television in particular presents an array of images in relation to death and the after-life through programmes such as *Touched by an Angel* and *Crossing Over*, to name but two.[14] Crawford and Rossiter (2003) have argued that because the media is so influential in the lives of children and young people, it is a framework commonly drawn upon in enabling them to weave together the different threads of meaning.

Weaving a sense of connectedness

In some instances, the children seemed to be weaving together the different strands of meaning as a means by which to connect to those who were significant to them, particularly those who were deceased. Michelle from the rural school wondered quite openly about her older sister, Kim, who had died when Michelle herself was quite young. Although deceased, Kim seemed to continue to be a part of Michelle's life. Michelle was able to weave together the threads of meaning to give expression to this relationship. She drew upon her peers' accounts of near death experiences among older family members to describe an occasion on which she herself had had an epiphany of Kim in her own life while at a favourite family holiday destination. She was able to describe in some detail the clothes Kim was wearing, and to comment on the surprise and happiness she felt in this encounter. For Michelle, this event was real and was clearly of significance for her. From this event, Michelle was able to create meaning and to foster her sense of connectedness with her deceased older sister, Kim.[15]

In this instance, it seemed that Michelle, and the other children who wondered about the deceased, had developed a sense of kinship between themselves and the dead. This accords with the findings of Hay and Nye (2006) in relation to the medieval qualities of spirituality that were suggested by the children in their particular study, and their relationship between the living and the dead. Hay and Nye noted that the religious practices of those living in medieval times intimate that people had a greater sense of kinship that seemed to extend not only across generational boundaries, but also across the boundary between the living and the dead. For example, the less wealthy depended in part on the financial support paid to them for the offering of prayers and attendance at Mass for the deceased person. In turn, the dead were viewed as being dependent upon the living in order that their souls could be adequately prayed for to ensure entry into heaven. Such interdependency then fostered a kinship-based sense of spirituality.

However, the children in my study seemed to be aware of this kinship not simply in terms of the deceased looking after them in times of difficulty or trouble. These children, particularly Michelle, seemed to have reached a heightened awareness of the relationship between themselves and the deceased for its own sake. Michelle, although quite young when her sister died, and in a sense would barely have known her, nonetheless seemed to have a profound relationship with her sister that, with the support of her family, had somewhat naturally formed. In this particular instance, the profound nature of this relationship could possibly be conceived of as the emergence of a Collective Self. Michelle appeared to experience an intimate sense of unity with Kim that exceeded the boundary between physical life and death, as did the other members of her family, a point which will be developed further in the next chapter. Each individual Self in this relationship was effectively unified. In other words, Self and Other had become one.

An Unresolved Tension

The emergence of the characteristic weaving the threads of meaning suggests that children of primary school age do in fact engage with and wonder about larger existential issues. This echoes the findings of other research in this field, particularly that of Coles (1990), Hart (2003), and Berryman (1991), who have all maintained that children are natural philosophers when reflecting on life's existential questions.

However, the emergence of this particular characteristic also presents some challenges for parents, and for teachers, particularly those involved in faith schools, where the mandate is to pass on to children the faith of the religious tradition which sponsors the school. Certain areas of the curriculum, in particular religious education, frequently explore the kinds of existential questions and wonderings that were present among the children in my research. There exists then, the opportunity for this curriculum area to tap into the natural wonderings of students, and to draw upon them in exploring and developing various topics. However, my research suggests that children's wondering leads them to draw from an eclectic range of frameworks in order that they can create meaning for themselves. They include, but are not limited to the Christian story. As such, the meaning-making and worldviews of students themselves in the classroom context cannot be ignored. This may present an enormous challenge for religious educators in faith contexts charged with the task of presenting and handing on a faith tradition. Is it possible to present, for example, the Christian message while at the same time honouring and taking seriously the worldviews of the children themselves?

This brings to the fore a tension which, perhaps, cannot be resolved. On the one hand, children have an ontological predisposition to create their own meaning, derived from the array of social and cultural frameworks available to them, and to construct a worldview based around their meaning-making. On the other hand, in taking into account the children's worldviews, some of which may be at odds with a particular faith tradition such as Christianity, religious educators in faith schools may need to offer an alternative framework of meaning. Does this imply then that children's meaning-making is to be manipulated and used as a stepping-stone towards a deeper understanding of the 'truth' according to a particular faith tradition's stance? This is a potentially dangerous proposition. At the very least it suggests the possibility that the worldview of a particular faith tradition could actually do violence to the worldviews of the children themselves. This is considered by many to be paramount to abuse, and is considered to be an infringement upon the rights of the child (see for example, Humanist Philosophers' Group 2001; Marples 2005).

The tension, then, can be seen as involving two quite different frameworks of meaning. First, it involves what might be described as a postmodern, or diatactical (Erricker 2001) frame in which children are free to engage with the complexity of interpretation, and to weave together their own threads of meaning. Second, the tension involves a religious frame in which learning entails the children in coming to see the 'truth' of the received and authoritative wisdom of the particular religious tradition.

Ota (2001) noted this inevitable tension, but proposed that it could be drawn upon in a creative and constructive way. One such way involves religious education, as a curriculum area, and learners in a process referred to as concerning *responsible partners*. While acknowledging that this term requires further unpacking, for religious education to act as a responsible partner and to contribute in a meaningful way to children's personal growth may require it to 'engage with pupils, allowing them to share their stories and to contribute to the community's story' (p.271). That is, religious education needs to partner children in entering the space between the authoritative wisdom of the faith tradition and the individually created meanings that offer personal significance for the children themselves. It is in this space that it must engage with children, exploring a range of frameworks of meaning including the Christian story. Herein exists a great tension and challenge for religious education. However, if this tension can be creatively addressed, religious education may contribute to children's spiritual development and creation of meaning.

For parents too, weaving the threads of meaning can present a challenge. Often a child may fashion a worldview, influenced by many frameworks of meaning, which is incompatible with the worldview of her or his parents, and can become a source of conflict as the child grows and matures. A great many arguments have erupted between children and their parents precisely because of the different worldviews held by each. For many parents, their worldview was created during a time characterized by modernity, when it was claimed that people came to understand the world by knowing its foundations – the large theories, or 'narratives' from which the rest of knowledge flows. Such foundations included science, economics, religion, and the like. Each foundation, or philosophical tradition had its own way of understanding the world, based in part on its views of how the world originated, what human beings are and how society is constructed. Today, children live in a postmodern world, in which those very foundational frameworks are questioned. In postmodernity, there is no one foundation for understanding the world. Instead there are a variety of different frameworks based on particular perspectives and viewpoints.[16] Children living in a postmodern context are only too aware of these many frameworks. For them, any one particular framework, or element thereof, is optional, and may be drawn upon in creating their own worldview. As a result, children's worldviews often differ considerably from those of their parents, causing at times considerable conflict. A popular phrase that was once used to describe this was 'the generation gap'. While this phrase may still bear some validity, I suggest that at the heart of much that has been described as simply a 'generation gap', is the conflict which results from the different worldviews that can be held by parents and their children.

In a Nutshell

- Weaving the threads of meaning refers to children's ability to draw upon their sense of wonder in order to make meaning of events and to piece together a worldview based around their attempts at meaning-making.

- In weaving the threads of meaning, children draw eclectically from a range of different frameworks of meaning. In effect, children enter the space between each of these different frameworks of meaning in order to select eclectically those elements which create meaning for themselves.

- Weaving the threads of meaning enables children to make meaningful connections with Self, Others, the world, and in some instances, with God.

- This characteristic can present challenges for parents, whose worldview may be significantly different from those being formed by their children, and for educators, particularly those working in faith contexts, where passing on a religious tradition could do violence to the worldviews held by the children themselves.

Some Guidelines for Nurturing Children's Ability to Weave the Threads of Meaning

Parents

- Become aware of, and develop a familiarity with the different frameworks of meaning from which your child derives meaning. These would include the media (particularly television), popular music, as well as their own lived experiences. Don't shy away from these. Discuss them with your child. Take an interest in them.

- Share your own frameworks of meaning with your child. This may present an alternative, or an additional source of meaning for your child. At the very least, if shared respectfully, these could create an opportunity for dialogue and conversation.

- Be sensitive: there may be times in which it is appropriate for you to accompany your child in entering the spaces between the many frameworks of meaning, and to act as a guide, or mentor; at other times, it may be more appropriate for your child to enter those spaces alone, so as to discern meaning for themselves.

- Be respectful, even when the worldviews being created by your child differ from those you hold. Show that you take your child's creation of meaning seriously, and be prepared to talk about this with your child.

Teachers

- Become familiar with the different frameworks of meaning from which children in your classroom appear to derive meaning. Be prepared to engage with those particular frameworks.

- Take seriously the way in which children have woven together the threads of meaning. These may become the starting point for addressing particular issues in the classroom, be they of a curricular or extracurricular nature.

- Where possible, draw on the worldview of the students as the starting point for planning your classroom curriculum, especially in subject areas such as religious education. One example of a curriculum document which encourages teachers to do this, and to take seriously the meaning-making systems of students is *Living Difference*, the Agreed Syllabus for religious education for Hampshire, Portsmouth and Southampton in the UK (Hampshire County Council, 2006).

- Explore ways in which you can act as a *responsible partner* in accompanying students in entering the spaces between the different frameworks of meaning.

- Consider how you might engage with students in religious education, whilst at the same time allowing them to share their own stories and allowing their stories to contribute to the community's story.

- Examine the curriculum documents that guide the planning for various subject areas (English, science, art, religious education, and so forth). Which suggested topics/units/modules could enable you to begin with the worldviews of the students themselves?

- Be conscious of minimizing the possible violence done to children's worldviews through the learning and teaching processes that are utilized.

- Be alert to opportunities within the curriculum for critiquing the frameworks of meaning drawn upon by children which may be potentially dangerous, particularly the media (television, popular music and the like). Critique advertisements, slogans, the lyrics of songs, and so forth.

CHAPTER 8

Spiritual Questing

The third group meeting in each of the three schools focused on the concept of value sensing (Hay and Nye 2006). Value sensing concerns the moral sensitivity of children. It includes a sense of that which really matters to the children themselves. The first phase of this group meeting entailed me sharing a short story with the children, and then inviting them to respond to the question of what really mattered to them. This responding was undertaken through both discussion, and, in the second phase of the meeting, a journal activity.

In response to the question, 'I wonder what you think really, really matters?' (Rebecca Nye, personal communication, 9 May 2002), and a follow-up question 'If you could have three wishes, I wonder what you might wish for?' the characteristic described in my study as *spiritual questing* became evident. This term has been adapted from the work of Horell (2003), who has suggested that the present time marks a broad cultural shift in the ways that people make sense of their lives and their world. Horell has described this movement as a shift away from the confidence of modernity towards the greater ambiguity and multiplicity of postmodernity. Emerging postmodern sensibilities, he has argued, give rise not to one, but to a range of attitudes towards life and the world. This range of attitudes is particularly evident in this young generation of children (and adolescents) known variously as 'Millennials' (Howe and Strauss 2000) and 'NetGen' (Hicks and Hicks 1999). Horell has used the term 'questing postmodernity' to describe one such attitude. The research described in this book has drawn on an adaptation of questing postmodernity, using the term spiritual questing, which seeks to promote 'imaginative creativity and the pragmatic construction of new patterns and self-identity' (Horell 2003, p.91). Spiritual questers view the shift from certainty towards a multiplicity of meanings as one of opportunity. Instead of resulting in skepticism, nihilism and trivializing in relation to human activity and thought, for spiritual questers, the current milieu provides opportunities for a freedom to envision more life-giving and life-enhancing ways of being.

Horell has noted that, in terms of the Christian tradition, those who might be classed as postmodern questers – spiritual questers in this present research – seek to explore new and perhaps more authentic ways of connecting with self, others, the earth and with God.[17]

Spiritual Questing

All group meetings provided much evidence of this characteristic of spiritual questing. The following reflective journal entry on Michelle in Year 5 in the rural school suggests the presence of this characteristic of spirituality. Michelle spoke freely about the keepsakes of her older sister Kim who had died when Michelle herself was quite young:

> When asked what it was that really mattered to her, Michelle's response was immediate. 'The stuff we have left of Kim, and mum's journal that says what we think about Kim and our grief that we've had inside,' she replied. 'When Kim died, dad and mum and I, and Tom did a bit too, we used to have a lot of dreams about Kim, and mum used to write them down in a journal. When we go on a big holiday, mum gives the journal to [a family friend] in case anything happens to the house while we're away.' She added, 'I've got a teddy bear that she used to love a lot, and some of her ornaments.'

The idea of a sense of connectedness after death seemed prevalent among this group of children, as was evidenced by Emily:

> 'I'd wish for everyone in my family who has died to come back so I can meet them,' said Emily. 'My grandpa died a long time ago, but he is important to me. Even though I didn't know him very well, I would still really like to meet him, like, probably, now.'

The counterparts of these children in Year 3 from the rural school also exhibited signs of spiritual questing. After a moment's thoughtful silence, when asked what really mattered to them, the children began to speak freely:

> Tom was the first to offer his thoughts. 'God and Jesus, and probably my family' he declared. 'My family cares for me and everything, and God and Jesus – because – I can't really explain, but they're kind of…' Tom's voice trailed as he searches for the language to convey his thoughts.
> 'Yeah, God and Jesus,' affirmed Michael, 'and Mary, because they're the kind of people that, if you could meet them, they'd be really nice. Also, my family and my pets matter to me.'
> 'What matters to me,' added Imelda, 'is to take care of my family because they might split up or have a divorce or something. You have to

take care of your family and they have to care for you, even if you do
something wrong, and even if they do something wrong to you. You still
have to care for them.'

Wallace, who had been thinking quietly, now took the conversation in
a slightly different direction. 'My life is important to me,' he declared,
'because the stuff I do is kind of daring, like mast windsurfing. I've got a
new board that's kind of big and fast and I hope I don't crash!'

Similarly, the following reflection on the Year 5 students in the inner city
school indicates spiritual questing as a characteristic of these children. When
asked what it was that really mattered to them, the following types of replies
were generated:

'Astrology,' replied May Ling.

[Other] responses came both instantaneously and simultaneously –
'It's star signs', 'And clairvoyance', 'Cancer, Capricorn...'

'They tell you about yourself and others,' replied Hy Sun reflectively.

I ask the question again. Ramsay, who had been relatively quiet, said
'Being myself... I like who I am.'

Missal affirmed his response, saying 'You're unique.'

'Imagine you had three wishes,' I began, 'What might you wish for?'

'Whenever I want something, it just comes to me!' offered Maria to
the sounds of further giggling.

'Like powers,' suggested Missal.

'Oooh, magic!' teased Hy Sun, waving his fingers like a magician...

'What kind of powers would you wish for?' I inquired.

Two responses again came instantaneously and simultaneously –
'Telepathy', 'That I can read minds'.

'That I can disappear whenever I want, when I'm embarrassed...'
continued Maria.

'Like on *Charmed*' clarified May Ling, alluding to a popular television
show that deals with magic and the occult.

'Yeah, and how Phoebe and Paige (characters from *Charmed*) use their
powers to save the universe!' added Missal enthusiastically. Ramsey and
May Ling nodded their heads in agreement.

Their counterparts in Year 3 of the inner city school also exhibited this characteristic of spiritual questing:

Almost as if reflecting to herself, Amina said 'I wish that I'm really, really
healthy and that my parents weren't divorced.'

Charlotte added 'I'd wish for a happy future, that my family stays
together, and that the poor become richer, well, not rich, but average, so

they don't.have to go around asking for money and that they live a good life.' This is the second time that Charlotte has indicated the importance of a happy future.

'Like, no one's poor in the world,' added Amina.

'Why might that be a good thing to wish for?' I probed.

'Cause it's doing something for another person,' replied Amina confidently.

Likewise, children in both value-sensing group meetings in the suburban school displayed the characteristic of spiritual questing. The following reflection on the Year 5 group meeting exemplifies the presence of this characteristic:

> John considered my request for information carefully, and responded by saying, 'Freedom really matters, because, a long time ago slavery was not illegal, and some people didn't have freedom, which everybody should be able to have.'
>
> 'Like the aborigines,' said Adam. 'They didn't have any freedom – they couldn't vote, they couldn't live wherever they wanted to.'
>
> 'But aborigines now can do anything that white people can do,' declared Cameron. 'Because we should treat all people the same way. And we should all have the same amount of the things we like.'

Again, searching for the right words was often difficult. As the conversation with this group of children continued, John indicated this difficulty in an explicit way:

> 'Love matters. If you weren't loved, I don't think any of us would be here, cos, you need love and affection, um – how shall I say this – some parents don't care about their children...' (John searches again for the right words). 'They don't send their children to school...they go away and leave their children to do the groceries and stuff. They don't care for them.'

Similarly, the Year 3 children in the suburban school exhibited the characteristic of spiritual questing:

> 'I would wish for world peace so that we could all be happy,' replied Stacey confidently.
>
> 'And that all the poor people have money and food and clothes,' added Zephaniah.
>
> 'I'd wish for no more war,' replied Sally, 'and that all the people who have been hurt or sick would get better.'

The Journal Activity

The children were also invited to respond through writing or drawing their responses in their journals, and, if they felt comfortable, to allow me to collect what they had written or drawn. This was an ethically sensitive moment in the research process. The children had been informed prior to commencing the task that I would, at the conclusion, invite them to allow me to have access to their journal entries, and it had been stressed that they could refuse this invitation. Evidence that the children did not feel compelled to accept this invitation was indicated by the fact that several chose to keep their journals private. In all, 28 of the 35 children allowed me to access their journal entries.

In examining these journal entries, it became apparent that there were many examples which suggested spiritual questing. Many of the entries contained either written or drawn references to the children's families and friendship groups as being what mattered most to them. In the suburban school, some of the Year 5 journal entries indicated that other issues were also of importance that could also be indicative of the notion of spiritual questing. The following two extracts from these entries illustrate this:

> I think that life matters a lot because obviously, without the gift of life, the whole world wouldn't exist. [The] trees and plants and sun and moon are all alive and they need warmth and water just like humans do. The world wouldn't be here because the world is made up from lots and lots of different things. Without life there probably wouldn't even be a universe and everything would just be black and there wouldn't be anything at all.
>
> What really, really matters is our religion. I think this because if we didn't have these we would definitely live a dull life. Our religions keep us going. They put strength in us.

Several of the journal entries collected contained lists of things that were indicative of spiritual questing. For example:

> Human beings, world peace, my family, God, Jesus (Year 3, suburban school).
>
> My health, my family, a happy future, no dangers in the world, nature, I don't die at an early age, my family not divorced (Year 3, inner city school).
>
> What matters to me is: the poor become healthy and they live a good life, we have peace in the world, the world becomes diplomatic, humans treat nature carefully, I don't become a bad person that takes drugs (Year 3, inner city school).

Books of astrology and stuff like tarot cards and powers. All my friends who are really close to me and my soft toy, Pookie Pookie (Year 5, inner city school).

Mum and dad, my pets, my grandma, grandpa, nana, Billy and Pa, my sisters and brothers, my life (Year 3 rural school).

As can be seen from both the children's own life expressions and their individual journal entries, spiritual questing, as a characteristic of children's spirituality in my particular study, entailed the children searching for authentic ways in which to relate with Self and Other.

A Reflection and Discussion on Spiritual Questing

Spiritual questing (along with weaving the threads of meaning to a lesser degree) was perhaps the most diverse characteristic to emerge in my study. Adapted from Horell's (2003) notion of questing postmodernity, spiritual questing promotes imaginative creativity, as well as the practical formation of self identity and ways of being in the world. For a spiritual quester, the present time provides opportunities for a freedom to envision more life-giving and life-enhancing ways of being. Horell notes that, in terms of the Christian tradition, those who might be classed as spiritual questers seek to explore new and perhaps more authentic ways of connecting with Self, others, the earth and with God. The children who participated in my research were questers. They were searching for genuine relationships with Self and beyond. Because there are potentially endless ways of achieving this, spiritual questing emerged in quite diverse ways in my research. For the ease of presentation, I have grouped these various ways together into 'themes' which seemed to indicate the children's spiritual questing.

Searching in their experience of Other

For some of the children, spiritual questing entailed a sense of Other and the relationship of Self with Other. At times this searching was in their experience of Other for a sense of life's meaning and purpose (Tacey 2003). In other instances, this searching was named explicitly as being in the Transcendent Other, for these children, God. For example, several children from the rural school indicated that one of the things that really mattered to them was a relationship with God and Jesus. While Tom from this group was less able to articulate and expand upon his thought in relation to this, Michael was able to describe in a little more detail this desired relationship in terms of actually meeting God, Jesus, and Mary, because, to use his own words, 'They'd be really nice.' In this instance, these two children were drawing upon religious language to search in their experience of and relation to the Transcendent for a sense of identity and life's meaning and purpose. This was particularly so, given that their responses were offered after a short time of quiet and contemplation in reply to my wondering about what really mattered to them. In searching their relationship to the Transcendent, these two children were possibly coming to a greater knowledge of themselves, since, without a relationship with an 'absolute other' (Tacey 2003, p.156), Self lacks a sense of identity, definition and form. In this instance, a part of their identity was possibly defined through their relationship with the Transcendent.

Family

In other instances, this searching was named as being in relation to family. Imelda indicated that her family really mattered, and that this mattering was unconditional. Regardless of what she had done, or what family members may have done to her, she considered families charged with the responsibility of caring for each of their members unconditionally. For Imelda, her family provided her with a sense of identity, and she in turn provided her family with a sense of definition and form.

Amina and Charlotte from the inner city school also indicated family as being something that mattered to them. For Charlotte, her family also provided a sense of identity and form. However, in Amina's case, her family had experienced breakdown through her parents' divorce. Almost reflecting to herself, Amina had said, 'I wish that my parents weren't divorced.' While her love for her parents, and their love for her might have remained unconditional, there was a sense in which Amina's definition of herself had been altered. She could no longer be defined by her family in quite the same way that perhaps she once was. Although she was continuing to search in her experience of her family for a sense of her identity, Amina seemed to realize that she would now also need to search elsewhere. The unifying bond that had held that family unit together had been severed, and although they remained connected to one another in various ways, the dynamic of the relationship was now different.

Michelle's relationship with her deceased older sister provides a further example of searching in her family for a sense of identity and definition. She was able to speak about the significance and value attached to the possessions of Kim that remained. The ornaments, the teddy bear, as well as the photographs and journal kept by Michelle's mother served as media through which Michelle, and indeed her whole family, could remain connected to Kim.

I had a strong sense through our conversations that Michelle's spiritual questing appeared to be actively seeking and exploring authentic ways of remaining connected with Kim. In this spiritual questing, it seemed that Kim defined who Michelle was, and reciprocally, Michelle defined Kim. While each child was a unique individual with her own particular likes and dislikes, and gifted with her own traits and talents, in terms of identity, it was almost as though without Kim, there was no Michelle, and without reference to Michelle, there was no Kim. They were unified in terms of a Collective Self in which the relationship of each to Other was inseparable in defining each other's being. It seemed that Michelle had an intuitive sense of this unity. Although she did not use language to express this, Michelle seemed to be intuitively aware of the Self-defining unity that she and her older sister shared.

This notion of defining, reciprocally, the relationship between the living and the dead accords with some of the findings of Coles (1990) in his interview with a young Hopi girl named Natalie. Coles reported that Natalie spoke of going to the mesa to visit her ancestors (mesa [maysa] is the term used for a flat elevated area. Found in South-western USA, it is a relatively flat area with steep sides. It is less extensive than a plateau). They held her, as if cradling her in a blanket, and they spoke to her, passing on the wisdom of what they had learned. Natalie was defined by her ancestors, and her ancestors were defined through reference to Natalie. It was a living sense of unity with Other which indicated the emergence of a Collective Self – Natalie and her ancestors were unified. Like Michelle in my own study, Coles suggests that Natalie too had a conscious awareness of this unity, although she did not necessarily possess the language to articulate it in these terms.

Fascination with the supernatural

Some of the children expressed their searching in relation to Other through what appeared as a fascination with the supernatural. This was particularly evident among the children from the inner city school. These children indicated that what really mattered to them were phenomena such as astrology, clairvoyance and the possession of supernatural powers. While some of the children indicated that these were simply fun or interesting to engage in, others placed a greater significance on them. Hy Sun said that astrology was important because it could tell you about yourself and others. While an interest in astrology, horoscopes and the like could be attributed to the peer group and media influences, it could also have been that these children believed that meaning and value in relation to one's Self and others could be found in one's zodiac sign, and in the terrestrial position of the stars. If taken seriously, this could inform about one's Self and about one's daily interactions with other people. Although they seemed somewhat reluctant to elaborate in great detail on their conceptions of astrology, it appeared clear that this phenomenon provided one source of their searching for meaning and purpose in life.

This same group of children also indicated that the possession of supernatural powers mattered to them. They seemed to have been greatly influenced by a popular television series titled *Charmed* which featured the notion of witchcraft. At first it seemed as though the children desired to possess such supernatural powers for their personal gratification. Maria had stated that these were important because she would be able to summon objects to herself whenever she wished to do so. She further went on to explain that the possession of such powers would enable her to disappear whenever she wished. However, further reflection upon this indicated something beyond personal gratification.

One of the features of the television series *Charmed* – and also of other media productions that were influential in these children's lives at that time, such as *Harry Potter* and *Lord of the Rings* – was the notion of good ultimately overcoming evil. Although the plots of these television series and films portrayed the many ways in which evil and destruction could run rampant, these were eventually and inevitably conquered by the good and virtuous. For example, in the Harry Potter movies, it is Harry himself who is the personification of good and overcomes evil. In *Harry Potter and the Philosopher's Stone* his trusted friend Hermione reminds Harry that he personifies the ultimate values that are sought after in life – friendship, loyalty, trustworthiness, and the like. Similarly the characters of Mr Frodo and Gandalf in *Lord of the Rings* personify that which is trustworthy and faithful in relation to their quest in spite of the evil and destructive forces at work. These qualities eventually overcome evil. The characters in the series *Charmed* operate in similar ways. Although the forces of evil seem to have acquired the upper hand, the good and virtuous ultimately overcome and succeed.

The children in my study too indicated an awareness of good overcoming evil. While they may not have possessed the language to express it in this way, and while they may have appeared to desire a possession of such supernatural powers for their own gratification, it seemed these children were seeking connection to a life force that promoted the life-giving values of the characters of these popular media dramas. These children were perhaps searching – questing – in Other for more life-enhancing ways of being in the world. What they were perhaps really seeking, what really mattered to them, was not necessarily the supernatural powers possessed by the characters of these films and television series, but rather the inherent values that these characters personified and lived out, and which in some instances were explicitly named either by the characters themselves, or by their associates. The supernatural was perhaps the media through which these children could access, or be in touch with these values. This could perhaps be seen in Missal's comment that she enjoyed the ways the characters of the series *Charmed* used their powers in such a way as to save others from evil. Other children in group also indicated their concurrence with Missal's thoughts by nodding their heads in agreement. Perhaps it was these values themselves that were of ultimate concern, but about which the children did not have a language that enabled them to give voice to them.

Affirming the Self

Another interesting feature of spiritual questing to arise among the Year 5 children in the inner city school was the affirmation and embodiment of Self. Amidst the discussion of astrology and the supernatural, Ramsey, who had been relatively quiet during the discourse, had stated that he liked being himself – that he liked who he was. In a sense, Ramsey was literally the physical embodiment of something that was of ultimate value – his own being. It was interesting to note that Ramsey did not intimate that he himself really mattered. Rather, it was the notion of *being* himself that was of importance, that is, his actual way of being in the world. 'I like who I am,' Ramsey went on to say. He seemed to understand that he embodied his own being. He liked who he was – an individual with his own particular likes and dislikes, thoughts, opinions and views. In short, he liked all of those features that distinguished him from others, and rendered him his own way of being in the world. He liked and was comfortable with his own Self.

Ramsey's peer, Missal, from this same group of children, also appeared to indicate that this notion of embodying and affirming one's own being was something that really mattered. While she herself did not indicate that she was necessarily comfortable with who she was – her own Self – Missal was quick to affirm Ramsey's statement: 'You're unique.' Missal had upheld Ramsey's embodiment of his own being and his way of being in the world. At the same time, she also indicated that the affirmation of one's own being was in fact something that really mattered to her. Her affirmation seemed genuine. It was possible in this short statement to glimpse something of Missal's searching for an authentic way of being and of relating to Other, in spite of her tendency to trivialize, as will be discussed in the following chapter. Although neither of these two children chose to elaborate further about this, these two basic statements – one a response to my wondering, the other an affirmation of the given response – reveal the spiritual questing of these two children through the embodiment of their sense of being. Perhaps both of these children were on the path to realizing their own true Selves – an understanding that accords with the descriptions of spirituality that have been offered in this book.

Altruism

In other instances, spiritual questing manifests itself in terms of the altruistic concerns of the children and their ability to empathize with others, especially those less fortunate. Charlotte and Amina both indicated that if they had three wishes, they would wish for the well being of the poor. They felt that they could do something for those less fortunate, albeit in the simple way of wishing them a better life. Amina added that it was important to wish such a thing because it was doing something for another person. These children appeared to show compassion and seemed to be able to empathize with those less fortunate.

Other children – Sally, Zephania and Stacey – also expressed this outward sense of connectedness with those less fortunate. Zephania wished that all the poor people in the world might have clothes and money. Both Stacey and Sally indicated that they would wish for the sick and the injured to be healed, and that there might be world peace. These altruistic notions were possibly a means of seeking and expressing their sense of connectedness with Other through their feelings of empathy and compassion. They were seeking more authentic and life-giving ways of being in the world. Rather than simply wishing for new toys or clothes, or for more money, in these instances the children were consciously expressing their genuine concern for other people. Their well-wishing for them served as a means by which they could facilitate a movement towards Other, and so could be understood to be an expression of their spirituality.

These altruistic notions accord with the descriptions of spirituality I have offered throughout this book – that spiritual awareness underpins altruistic and ethical behaviour, and therefore that spirituality may be given expression outwardly in terms of the way in which one acts towards Other. These children appeared to be able to empathize with and express compassion towards those less fortunate than themselves, and expressed this in terms of action – of doing something that they as young children could realistically do – to wish well for them.

A concern for the larger themes of life

The other key way in which spiritual questing manifesed itself was through the children's concern for what I have called the larger themes and values of life. These themes particularly included freedom and love. When asked what it was that really mattered to him, John from the suburban school seemed to consider my request for information carefully. He indicated that freedom was something of ultimate concern. It was clear that this child valued his own freedom and did not take it for granted. He was able to empathize with those who could not share in this basic human right. For John, and indeed for his peers, freedom was considered to be an entitlement for all people. Adam in this same group of children added to John's views by reminding both his peers and myself that it was only in recent times that particular groups of people, such as the Australian aboriginal community, gained access to basic rights to freedom.

Love was also a theme which was considered as being something that really mattered. Perhaps from his own experiences, John from the suburban school indicated his understanding of the love between a parent and a child as an expression of connectedness to Other. While experiencing some difficulty in finding the language to articulate his thinking, John also expressed a sense of empathy for those children who do not experience the love of a parent. He has stated '…some parents don't care for their children…they go away and leave their children to do the groceries.' John was revealing something of his heartfelt values that really mattered to him. His spirituality was given expression as a sense of connectedness with those who may not have experienced love in the way that he had through his compassion and empathy. Through the theme of love, John was able to give expression not only to something of ultimate concern, but also to his sense of connectedness with Other.

The immediate temporal horizon

My reflection upon spiritual questing gave rise to the notion that the present time in which these children were situated actually abounds with opportunities for spiritual questing. Horell (2003) has noted that the current milieu, characterized by postmodernity and its multiplicity of meanings, presents many opportunities for those who seek new and authentic ways of relating to others and of being in the world. For instance, the children in Year 5 from the inner city school in my study indicated that they were searching in the supernatural, in astrology and in clairvoyance for a sense of meaning and purpose. The present temporal horizon enabled and encouraged this searching to take place. Whereas once, a time characterized by a more classical worldview might have clearly indicated where one was to look for a sense of life's meaning and purpose, particularly in the religious sphere, the present time, distinguished by its plurality of meanings, seemed to give licence to these children to search among alternative sources. A multiplicity of meanings suggests that there is no one objective reality. Meaning, for these children, could be found and created from within their specific life contexts.

In a similar way, and as suggested also by the characteristic weaving of the threads of meaning, the immediate temporal horizon gave licence for many of the children in my research to quest by creating their own sense of meaning. They did not limit themselves to any one particular reality, but chose eclectically from a range of narratives in their searching for meaning and a sense of connection to Other. The time in which these children found themselves historically enabled and encouraged them to search among an array of narratives and to choose elements from them. The children were in no way apologetic for doing this. They saw it as a legitimate act which, using my own terminology, was effectually validated by the particular time in history in which they were situated.

However, this searching did not appear to be a random or arbitrary act. It was not, as some may suggest, a 'spirituality supermarket' (Crawford and Rossiter 2006) in which the children sought out elements from these frameworks of meaning as commodities which could be discarded when their usefulness was outgrown. Neither was it a case of 'whateverism', the term that Hughes (2007) employs to describe the way in which some young people appear to put together their worldview. Both of these notions suggest a haphazard and arbitrary type of searching, and almost that the resultant product will be disposable when it outgrows its use, just as the products we buy and consume from the supermarket are disposable. Perhaps there is a sense in which the present temporal horizon may function as a time of disposability. However, the questing on the part of the children in my research appeared to be far more intentional, albeit subjective, as evidenced by the reflection and thought that had gone into their responses. The temporal milieu in which these children were historically located played a part in enabling this intentional, deliberate searching. While it neither affirmed nor refuted the efforts of their seeking, or the products of their seeking, the time functioned so as to enable and encourage their searching. That is not to say that what they have sought through their questing is necessarily the end product. As they grow, mature, and encounter new experiences and new frameworks, my instinct is that, rather than discarding the result of their initial questing, they will incorporate and accommodate the products of their subsequent searching into their worldview, so that it continues to have meaning for them. Methodologically, of course, this cannot be proven. However, if nothing else, this indicates the need for further research that focuses on the way in which children create and continue to seek meaning in order to authentically relate to both the human and nonhuman worlds.

In a Nutshell

- Adapted from the Horell notion of 'questing postmodernity', spiritual questing involves the seeking to explore new and perhaps more authentic ways of connecting with Self, others, the earth and, for some, with God.

- Spiritual questers view the shift from certainty towards a multiplicity of meanings as one of opportunity.

- For spiritual questers, the present time provides opportunities for a freedom to envision more life-giving and life-enhancing ways of being.

- The children in my research indicated their spiritual questing through their experience of Other, through family, through a fascination with the supernatural, through altruism, and through a concern for the larger themes of life.

Some Guidelines for Nurturing Children's Spiritual Questing

Spiritual questing entailed the children searching for meaning and for ways of being in the world. Their responses to the question 'I wonder what you think really, really matters?' indicated the many and varied paths of their seeking for authentic ways to relate to Self and Other. The time in which today's children seek, sometimes described as postmodern, seems to be encouraging and affirming of their efforts to explore new ways of being in the world. Again, there are many challenges here. Some possible ways in which children's spiritual questing might be nurtured are listed below:

- Parents and teachers support children in their spiritual questing.

- Affirm children as being who they are. Allow them to embody their own way of being in the world.

- Parents and teachers appropriately and sensitively act as guides in this process of children's spiritual questing, especially in light of the fact that much of this questing occurs in realms outside of what may once have been considered to be the foundational worldviews.

- Become familiar with some of the ways and places in which children search for a sense of life's meaning and purpose. Do not shy away from these.

- As adults, we need to identify those things that really matter to us. What is it that is of ultimate value or concern for us? Do these parallel with some of the things that really matter to our children?

- There is much research to suggest that, for many young people in Western culture, institutional religion no longer offers or provides the answers for spiritual questers (see for example Drane 2000; Hughes 2007). This seems to be true for children also, who, as my own research suggests, often search in places outside of the realm of traditional faith. Yet, their questing is genuine. Those things that really mattered to them indicated that the children were actively seeking new and authentic ways of being and of relating to others, albeit that their searching was sometimes leading them in alternative directions. There is a need for parents and educators to provide appropriate spaces in which searching can take place. Does the classroom provide a space that is conducive for spiritual questing? Can an environment be established in the home in which children feel free to search, and yet are guided and supported in that process?

- In planning for the classroom religious education programme, try to incorporate opportunities for spiritual questing to occur.

- Give children time for moments of solitude and silence during the day. A consideration of those things that are of ultimate value and meaning requires times of silence.

- Take advantage of quiet places throughout the school. Many primary schools have established quiet places – garden areas, multipurpose areas and the like. Utilize these spaces for reflection and meditation.

- Ask children to name and to focus on others for whom they may feel compassion and empathy.

- Provide opportunities to use journals as a means by which to engage with issues of meaning and value. As shown in my study, these can provide a valuable means by which students can work through and articulate their thoughts and feelings in relation to those things that really matter. Remember, however, that for a journal to be effective, the contents need to be confidential – that is, 'for the students' eyes only'. Any attempt to collect them, to read them or to 'correct' them, invades the students' sense of privacy, and the activity will cease to have any real benefit. The students will record only what they perceive the educators wants to read – the exception being if a student *chooses* to share her or his reflections with the teacher. Even here, ethical sensitivity is required. Is the student freely choosing to share a journal entry, or does the student perceive this to be a requirement of the activity?

- In her book, *The Soul of Education*, American educator Rachel Kessler (2000) identifies seven 'gateways' to the soul of young people. The second and third of these gateways – the longing for silence and solitude, and the search for meaning and purpose – could be used by teachers as themes around which to facilitate spiritual questing.

CHAPTER 9

Factors that Inhibit Spirituality

This chapter presents a discussion of and reflection upon each of two factors that appeared to inhibit the children's expression of their spirituality.[18] The identification of these factors were particularly evident during the value sensing group meetings, where the children were invited to respond to the questions 'I wonder what you think really, really matters?' and 'If you could have three wishes, I wonder what you might wish for?' Although each of these questions generally resulted in the children's spiritual questing, as was attested to in the previous chapter, two particular factors emerged which appeared to act so as to restrict the children to their superficial, or outward self, rather than enabling them to move towards their true Self, or allow their true Self to surface. Although I did not set out in my study to identify those elements that may inhibit expressions of children's spirituality, they nonetheless arose as an unexpected, but significant finding. I have included them here because they signal to parents, teachers, and others who work with children, realities which may emerge to counter the nurturing of spirituality.

The particular factors identified in my study which appeared to inhibit the children's expression of their spirituality were material pursuit and trivializing.

Material Pursuit

The characteristic termed as material pursuit suggested that the children genuinely believed that what mattered most to them was the acquisition of money and/or material possessions. For instance, when asked what really mattered to them the Year 3 children from the inner city school responded as follows:

> Marco and Tran immediately interjected. 'My computer!' 'TV!' They shouted almost simultaneously.
>
> Ali thought momentarily and then replied, 'Nothing – OK, money!'

At this, Amina, who was growing impatient with her classmates' seemingly trivial responses, asked 'What about food? You wouldn't be alive if you didn't eat food or drink water. What about McDonalds? Isn't that important to you?'

Ali shook his head. He was determined. 'If I can get enough money,' he began, 'I can buy everything. I'd spend ten dollars every day.'

At this, Tran declared, 'I'd wish for more money – I always ask for my mum's money.'

There was also evidence of material pursuit among the Year 5 children in the inner city school, as the following reflective journal entry indicates:

'I wonder what you think really, really matters', I probed.

Slowly, even reluctantly, some responses were offered – soft toys, music, books. Yet, when I inquired as to whether the children might like to say something about these, there was an awkward silence, and a sense of uneasiness.

I wondered if they could have three wishes what they might wish for.

'I'd wish for money,' declared Fadde, 'so that I can be rich and buy whatever I want.' The other children nodded in agreement. I could sense that this was not a comment made in jest. Fadde seemed to be quite serious – and so did his classmates. In a moment of honesty and genuine response to my question, it seemed that money was that which was of value and importance.

Similarly, the following reflection, this time from Year 3 students from the rural school, indicates the presence of material pursuit. When asked what they might wish for if granted three wishes, the following replies ensued:

'To get a horse,' replied Susan quickly, almost struggling to give voice to the many possible wishes that were entering her mind at a rapid rate of knots, 'and to get lots of money for a holiday just for me!'

'I would wish for a motor bike,' added Imelda thoughtfully, 'and to get a new car – if I was allowed to get a car – and to buy a bigger farm.'

Michael said that he would like to make it to the AFL (Australian Football League) and to win a medal. While Wallace, reflecting briefly for a moment, declared that he would wish to be the best at windsurfing and skiing, as well as to get a licence to drive his first motor bike.

These reflections indicate that the responses of these children were serious. They were being honest. The more they were probed, even by their peers, they more they indicated a genuine belief in materialism as that which mattered most to them. Material possessions may serve a purpose in that they can contribute to the defining of one's identity and sense of belonging. For instance, Maslow's (1970b) motivation theory suggested a hierarchy of human needs corresponding to growth and maturity. Maslow claimed that there are five levels of needs that all people experience. The four lower levels are grouped together as deficiency needs. These include: physiological needs – food, water, sleep; safety needs – security, shelter; belonging needs – love, companionship, relationships; and esteem needs – self respect, self esteem. Maslow argued that the higher being needs can only come into focus once the lower needs have been satisfied. When the human person's most basic needs are met – food, clothing, shelter, and the like – other higher needs emerge. It is pertinent to note that a damaging or destructive event in a person's life may cause regression to the lower needs. In applying Maslow's theory to the case of the particular children in my study, it may have been that only when their need to belong and their need to define their identity was met that they may then begin looking beyond towards their inner Self for a sense of that which really matters. However, in these instances, the materialistic desires were satisfying the children's outer self, that is, the ego. They did not seem to have yet moved beyond this need. This is consistent with a consumerist culture which continually promotes the outer self and its desires. Material pursuit then appeared to be a factor that inhibited these children's expression of spirituality because the searching for what really mattered remained solely at the outer level. The true Self was not engaged.

A Reflection and Discussion on Material Pursuit

Relationship with the material

Material pursuit seemed to exhibit itself among the children as a preference to relate to possessions and material wealth rather than to people. This was particularly evident among the Year 3 and Year 5 children from the inner city school, and among the Year 3 children from the rural school. Among these children, particularly both groups from the inner city school, there seemed to be a sense of mistrust of others, and reliance upon the superficial self and upon whatever might satisfy the ego. Although snippets of the conversation among these children indicated a wish to connect with Other in relationship and to explore the larger existential questions of ultimate importance, in many cases, the children seemed to succumb to the materialistic desires of the ego, despite the impulses of the inner Self to move towards the Collective Self. For example, among the Year 3 children from the inner city school Marco, Tran and Ali insisted that computers, television and money were ultimately important to them, in spite of Amina's suggestion that there might be more important things in life. Tran had further stated that he would wish for 164 TVs so that he could watch 164 programmes at once. He also wished that he was the richest man in the world and the king of the whole world. Ali from this same group had stated that if he could have enough money, he could buy anything he wanted. Similarly, Fadde in Year 5 from the inner city school declared that money was the most important thing for him. There seemed to be a reliance on the superficial self, and on the spending power of the self, rather than a sense of connectedness with Other.

For many of these children, there was possibly a sense in which they felt that a 'relationship' with the material could offer a greater degree of contingency. A relationship with the material could somehow be trusted more than a relationship with people. For example, money is a commodity that one either has or does not have. It is not ambiguous. A PlayStation, a television set, a computer game comprise material possessions that, once acquired, remain constant, at least in the eyes of these children. Relationships with people, on the other hand, possess an inherent element of risk and uncertainty. One needs to be able to reveal something of Self to Other, thereby leaving one vulnerable to potential ridicule and scorn. The children in both groups from the inner city school seemed to be aware of this reality, perhaps from personal experience. It seemed as though this was territory into which they did not again wish to venture, at least, not with those of their peers who were present during the value-sensing group meetings. If one has already experienced a relationship in which the bonds of trust and mutual respect have been damaged through teasing, ridicule, abandonment and the like, then one is perhaps inclined to be mistrustful and wary. Perhaps one may be predisposed to placing trust in those things that appear unambiguous and which cannot disappoint. It seemed that the longer that one places trust in the material, the more genuine one appears to be about this as a source of ultimate value. This inhibited the children's expression of spirituality and movement towards unity with Other.

For these particular children, it seemed that scientific advances and technology, particularly in the form of computer games, had hampered their social interaction with other people, thereby impeding the path towards a consciousness of the Collective Self. Certainly, social interaction and the ability to be able to enter into relationship with Other could be considered as contributing towards a sense of well being and resilience. For instance, Mountain (2004) identified that children's sense of connectedness, particularly with their family and peer group, is central in building resilience, a quality that is necessary to combat the stresses and problems that most children are confronted with in the postmodern world. Consequently, the findings here suggest that parents, teachers and others who work with children need to be aware of and respond to the possible impact of technology on the lives of children who do not know a world without it.

A late capitalist consumerist culture

Material pursuit became evident as a factor that inhibited the children's expression of their spirituality in a time characterized by what Mercer (2004) has referred to as late capitalist consumerist culture. These children were (and are) living in a time in which society on the one hand appears to support and affirm children with material excess, while at the same time ignoring, or doing harm to their spiritual needs through neglect of their basic requirements, such as their need for unconditional love, their desire to belong, or an affirmation of their inherent worth as human beings. Further, in this consumerist milieu, the notion of children's consumer behaviour has become a trend in Western culture. Not only can children spend their own money, but they are capable of influencing the spending of their parents. They constitute a future market. They are a group of people with purchasing power who, as children, are 'ripe for the establishment of brand loyalty and the development of consumer behaviors that will shape how they spend money as adults' (Mercer 2004, p.7).

The consumerist milieu in which these children were growing up places an importance upon the acquisition of money and wealth as being the norm. The influence of the media in suggesting that it is necessary to purchase the latest in a particular fashion or trend, or the best in an item of electrical or household furniture in order to belong, or to 'fit in' impacts upon the value that is ultimately placed upon those items, particularly those that are desired, but which are financially beyond reach. The time in which these children found themselves was one in which they were effectively consumers in training. They have begun their 'consumership' at an early age. Further, it has been noted that when one grows up with consumerism from infancy, one comes to assume its own logic and normalcy (Stearns 2001).

The effects of this consumer time in which children live and the inhibiting effect upon their expression of spirituality could be seen in some of the many responses to the question, 'Imagine you had three wishes, what might you wish for?' For example, Susan in Year 3 from the rural school replied that she would wish for a horse, for lots of money and for a holiday just for herself. She appeared to struggle to give voice to her many possible wishes as they seemed to enter her mind so rapidly. There was a sense in which the consumer choice was almost overwhelming. There was an excitement in this as the many possibilities of consumer choice forged their way into the consciousness of this child, almost like a rush of adrenalin. Similarly, Wallace in this same group wished for a licence to drive his first motorbike, as well as to be the best at windsurfing and skiing – two leisure activities that would be considered expensive to maintain. There was no shortage of possible consumer choices. The children's thought process seemed to be almost instantaneous. It was as if their minds had become suddenly awash with the possibilities of what they could wish for to satisfy the consumer drive.

This temporality served to impact in a destructive way upon the spirituality of the children. Having grown to understand consumerism as the norm, that which was of ultimate value to them was, in some cases, perceived to be the acquisition of material possessions, and the spending power to purchase that which they believed might fulfil their desire. Fuelled by the influences of the media and their peers, these children appeared to often place their value of consumerism at the expense of human relationship with others. Their sense of connectedness – indeed unity – was being sought not in Other, but rather through the material.

A dangerous, yet enticing space

The space in which this inhibiting factor emerged could be considered a dangerous space. It was, in some instances, a space of suspicion and mistrust. It was a space that seemed to actively encourage the children to search elsewhere for a sense of connectedness, and appeared to be successful in doing so. It was a space where the children's lack of trust and wariness in terms of being accepted by their peers led to their desire and action for acceptance through the possession of material things. Potentially, this is a nihilistic and materialistic alternative. It was a space in which the pursuit of material acquisition was valued and seen as that of ultimate importance. This seemed to occur at the expense of genuine human relationships. It appeared also that this was an inescapable space. These children had been raised with images of consumerism from an early age. They had, as noted, effectually become consumers in the making in a space that had been created and that was conducive to this purpose. At the same time, it was a space from which some of these children expressed little desire to escape. For example, Marco and Tran in Year 3 from the inner city school seemed quite contented in their attachment to their computer games and television viewing. It was almost as though there was no reason for them to wish to seek an alternative space in which to be. Similarly, some of the other children in this study – Wallace and Susan in Year 3 from the rural school – seemed to be satisfied with this space in which they found themselves. For these children this space was normal. They had known no other. Having grown up with consumerism from infancy, this space had taken on the appearance of normality.

This could be interpreted as children seeking identity and a sense of belonging through their material possessions. As noted, Maslow's (1970b) motivation theory indicates that until the basic needs of an individual are met, higher needs will not emerge. In this instance, the basic needs of these children, in terms of food, water, and a secure home were mostly met, which led them to another level, the search for belonging outside their immediate family unit, a factor necessary for their sense of identity and self. It would appear that their material possessions had a role in the process. These objects provided them with a sense of identity as well as a sense of belonging, since to acquire these possessions was to 'fit in' with both the peer group and society. These material possessions, then, could satisfy the concerns of the outer self. Once these needs had been met, there was a possibility that the children may have been in a position to identify those things that really mattered to them, and so be in a position to move beyond the outer self to discover the true Self. However, to achieve this, guidance and mentoring may be necessary. Guidance would be required in order to enable these children to move from the outer to the true Self.

Although this was a space lurking with hidden dangers, it was at the same time an enticing space. The possibility of wealth and consumer choice carried with it a certain temptation and excitement. It was a space in which the children could dream of having their material desires fulfilled. Perhaps in this sense it was an escapist space. It was a space to which the children could retreat from the mistrust and experiences of hurt from others by placing instead their hope – their trust – in the promise of material, or consumer fulfilment. Evidence of this could be seen in the almost immediate responses of the children to the question 'Imagine you had three wishes, I wonder what might you wish for?' The invitation to enter a space in which to dream about the fulfilment of their materialistic desires was almost too good to be true. They did not need to be asked a second time. The children seemed to take full advantage of the invitation, and, in some instances, were for a brief time almost overwhelmed by the infinite possibilities presented to them.

A lack of embodiment

Material pursuit could also be portrayed by a lack of embodiment, or at least a reluctance to embody a sense of meaning and value in relation to Other. In the case of the children in Years 3 and 5 from the inner city school, it seemed as though some of their previous experiences had led their felt sense to intuit the mistrust present in those particular situations. These bodily sensations may have remained a vivid reality for those children, so much so that they came to the fore of their consciousness in these value sensing group meetings, and in fact, whenever they experienced situations in which they sensed a mistrust of others. For example, the constant sniggering and the awkward silences particularly among the Year 5 children from the inner city school may have indicated that these children were again sensing the air of mistrust among the group. Rather than embody those values that might lead them to connect in relationship with others, particularly their peers, these children seemed to choose instead to embody a desire and a preoccupation with materialism. They appeared to physically withdraw from their peers and from the space of mistrust to express their reliance upon the self and their pursuit of the material that, in their eyes, might provide the contingency they were seeking.

Several of the children in Year 5 from the inner city school indicated that what they believed really mattered to them were their soft toys, music and books. These items, it seemed, may have been used to replace the connectedness and possible relationships with those they did not trust. It is possible to imagine each of these children in the quiet and privacy of her or his own bedroom curled up on the bed with a soft toy, or quietly reading a novel, or listening to the music pounding through the headphones of a Walkman. Each of these would be considered tactile experiences. Not only that, they are solitary experiences. There is no compulsion to connect with others in relationship. There tends to be a reliance only on the self and upon that which satisfies the self.

There may also have been a sense in which the soft toy became a projection of themselves. The children were seeking someone they could trust. Because of their reliance upon the self, they may have felt that they could trust themselves. The soft toy, as a projection of themselves then became something that was trusted, and perhaps relied upon. It is possible to imagine these children confiding in a teddy bear of some kind, telling it those things they dare not reveal to anybody else. When viewed in these terms, it can be seen that these items then became treasured among what really mattered to the children. The value of them was possibly immeasurable.

Trivializing

The second of these inhibiting factors has been termed trivializing. This is an adaptation of 'trivializing postmodernity', a term used by Horell (2003) in describing one particular attitude amongst the range of those held by people in the present milieu. 'Trivializing postmodernity' highlights the fact that the more people come to realize that universal understanding is not achievable, the more likely it is that they may be forced to accept a quite limited sense of what can hoped for in their personal and communal lives. Such attitudes then advance skepticism, nihilism and trivializing in relation to human activity and thought. Horell, cites the example of *Seinfeld*, one of the most highly rated television programmes of recent times in popular culture about a group of people who lead trivial and 'do nothing' lives, as an example of trivializing postmodernity.

In my research, trivializing referred to the avoidance of confronting issues of meaning and value in life, as well as to the making light of such issues. Evidence of this inhibiting factor of spirituality was particularly apparent in two group meetings, where the children indicated a distinct discomfort in talking about those things that really mattered to them. In many cases, and in the absence of an adequate language to express their ideas, the children seemed to prefer to dismiss that which was too difficult or awkward to speak about by trivializing. The following reflective journal entry on the Year 5 children from the inner city school serves as an example of trivializing.

As these children set about the journaling task of writing/drawing what it was that really mattered to them, Missal frowned. She, like the other children, was finding it difficult to communicate issues of meaning and value. She engaged in some idle chatter and giggling. 'This chair is uncomfortable,' she complained. 'I haven't got a pencil,' she protested. The other children too made similar remarks. Although snippets of their earlier conversation indicated that there was a need and a wish to engage at a deeper level…it seemed easier to trivialize and mask their deeper feelings by a façade of idle chatter and giggling.

Hesitantly, they attempted the task. Fadde was busily drawing and writing, and stated, almost as if thinking out loud, 'Money.'

At this Missal turned to him and said 'Money's not important.'

'Yes it is,' replied Fadde. 'You can buy anything.'

'You can't buy love,' retorted Missal. She was serious, but as the other children began to snigger at her remarks, she too began to smile and laugh, almost as if realizing that she has momentarily broken her façade.

> Lines from a song on a recent episode of a popular television series were then taken up in chorus by the children...

Similarly, the following reflective journal entry on the Year 3 children from the inner city school may also serve as an example of trivializing. When asked what it was that really mattered to them, three of the children, Marco, Tran and Ali, appeared to look uncomfortable. They looked away from me and began to fidget. Marco began tapping a pencil. Tran, who was fidgeting with an eraser, seemed clearly embarrassed:

> There followed a lengthy and awkward silence during which the children continued to avoid eye contact with one another as well as with myself. They seemed to be experiencing a physical discomfort in response to this silence in the face of issues of ultimate meaning and value.
>
> There was a sense in which the children also appeared to be perplexed by my question. It was as though they were unsure of exactly what it was that was being asked of them. It was almost as though they did not know how to respond, and so preferred to remain silent.
>
> 'What about you, Ali?' I asked, noticing that Ali too appeared restless and almost reluctant to contribute.
>
> He thought for a moment. 'Nothing – I can't think of anything that's important to me,' replied Ali shrugging his shoulders.

A Reflection and Discussion on Trivializing

A façade

It appeared that in some instances the children had effectively masked their inner feelings and values by generating a façade of giggling, idle chatter, and short comical remarks that 'made light' of any attempt to explore ultimate values. Perhaps over time, a sense of mistrust had emerged among them, and this façade served as a means by which each could protect herself or himself from the possible ridicule and teasing from peers. It seemed that the only way these children could relate to one another was through this façade, which inhibited any possible movement towards Ultimate Unity (de Souza 2004, 2006). It thus acted in a destructive way upon their expression of spirituality. There were, however, times in which it was possible to see through the veneer. For example, Missal in Year 5 from the inner city school stated, in reply to Fadde's comment about money as being of ultimate value, that 'You can't buy love.' Momentarily, Missal had taken off her mask, and had revealed to her peers something that was of genuine value to her – love. She placed a value on love that could not be equated in monetary terms, and this was something that was of ultimate importance to her. However, her peers seemed unable, or perhaps unwilling, to relate to Missal in this way. This comment was somehow socially unacceptable among the peer group. Both the other children and Missal sensed that there had been a breaking of convention. As her peers began to snigger, Missal too retreated behind the safety of the façade, and she too began to trivialize her comment by giggling and making light of what she had said.

This notion of a façade created by the children as a means through which they seemed to relate to one another is pertinent. In drawing upon Carl Jung's exploration of the archetype, the work of Helminiak (1996) sheds some light upon this inhibiting factor of trivializing, and upon the notion of the façade created by the children in masking their values. All human beings possess a desire to belong and to live in relationship with others. Helminiak maintained that a requirement of this desire is for one to adapt one's own aspirations and inclinations to those of others. Becoming a member of any group, be it family, friends, school or work implies a process of socialization. While this process enables one to share in the wealth of learning and culture that is proper to one's society, it also involves a person surrendering something of her or his uniqueness. Helminiak has maintained that the reality of this human process manifests itself in the personality of the individual through the archetypes of *persona* and *shadow*.[19]

As an archetype, persona refers to the social role that each person plays in order to fit into the particular group to which she or he belongs. The persona is the front, the façade, or the social presentation that structures a person's interactions with others. It parallels the notion of the superficial self discussed throughout this book. As a necessary element of being human, the persona is natural. In as much as a person acts authentically when acting out their persona, it becomes a concrete form in which a person expresses herself or himself in the world. However, when the persona prevents a person from acting authentically, it may become a liability because it exerts excessive control over a person's life.

Helminiak (1996) argued that the shadow is the underside of the persona. It refers to those under-prized aspects of a person which socialization has pushed into the background. It refers to those features of thought, behaviour and the like that are considered socially unacceptable or suspect within the particular group or social structure to which one belongs. However, this does not mean that such aspects are malevolent. Socialization often relegates some of a person's most unique gifts or talents to the shadow because they challenge the established societal forms. For example, a person's creativity, high level of achievement, or their intelligence may be consigned to the shadow because, in some way, they are considered to threaten or undermine the social structure of the group, or even the society.

The shadow then is a threat to the persona. Those feared and repressed aspects of an individual continually surface, demanding to be heard. However, their expression challenges the individual's established role and attempted complacent self-image. In a healthy personality, the shadow and the persona play off against each other. They contribute to an unfolding and to a depth and richness of life. However, as noted, if there is not a balance between the shadow and the persona, and the latter assumes too much control, it may prevent a person from acting authentically.

This sheds some light upon the inhibiting factor of trivializing as exhibited by the Year 3 and Year 5 children from the inner city school in my study, particularly in Missal's response to Fadde's obsession with money. 'You can't buy love,' retorted Missal. Her persona – her façade – had initially been in keeping with her established role among her group of peers. Her sense of mistrust had led both her and her companions to present an outward showing of complacency and of being superficial. Social pressure, it seemed, had demeaned the deeper issues of meaning and value – at least among the peer group – to the shadow. This was evident in their reluctance to engage in conversation about what really mattered to them, choosing instead to trivialize by giggling, by making facetious comments, and by avoiding the invitation to write or draw about their ultimate values. However, in Missal could perhaps be seen something of the shadow attempting to surface, demanding to be heard. Fadde's talk about money seemed to activate the shadow, forcing it to surface almost in a way over which Missal had little control. It had been repressed, but now exploded in her statement, 'You can't buy love.' The shadow, albeit momentarily, had surfaced and threatened her persona. Such an admission of the importance of love on the part of Missal may have been unacceptable, even suspect in the social situation in which she found herself – that of her peer group. The collective persona of her peer group then set about repressing the shadow, and her companions began to snigger. Missal's persona then also set about repressing the shadow which had begun to manifest itself, by making light of the comment, and restoring the façade. The social role played by Missal in fitting into her peer group had been reinstated. This was an instance in which Missal's persona exerted too much influence, preventing her from acting authentically. Missal's shadow had challenged the accepted norms of her social circle, and aside from a brief moment, it would have seemed that in this instance the persona emerged victorious.

Similarly, among the Year 3 children from the inner city school, the notions of persona and shadow were active. For example, when Ali was pressed a little further in conversation relating to what really mattered to him, his persona initiated the most indicative reply of trivializing. He shrugged his shoulders, replying, 'Nothing... I can't think of anything that is important to me.' In this instance, his shadow did not appear to surface.

Amina from this same group of students, however, seemed to indicate that her shadow was demanding to be heard. In response to her peers' materialistic responses, she asked, 'What about food? You wouldn't be alive if you didn't eat food or drink water.' While this comment was perhaps not as compelling as that of her Year 5 counterpart Missal, it did suggest Amina recognized another dimension in the basic necessities of life and survival. It seemed that she was attempting to inject a level of seriousness into the triviality of the discussion. Further, Amina did not seem to be inhibited in any way by challenging her peers in this way. Her shadow had manifested itself, and seemed to have successfully challenged the persona. In this instance Amina was able to act authentically. There appeared to be a balance in the playing off of her persona and shadow, resulting in a healthy personality. Her peers did not snigger or make light of her comment. Rather, they simply restated and justified their own position, remaining at the superficial level. For example, Ali responded to her by stating, 'If I can get enough money...I can buy everything.'

A space of mistrust, awkward silence and ambiguity

The type of space in which trivializing emerged could be described as a space of mistrust of the Other. While this is not to suggest that all the spaces in which these children entered could be characterized in this way, it seemed that the particular space that had been created during the value sensing group meetings of the Year 3 and Year 5 children from the inner city school, was at times one of mistrust and suspicion. The mistrust appeared to emerge in relation to the peer group. It seemed that within this space, the children were often reluctant to speak about issues of meaning and value for fear of the reaction that would be encountered from their companions. Evidence of such a reaction could be seen particularly among the Year 5 children from the inner city school, who constantly sniggered and made light of the comments of each other. Perhaps this sense of suspicion and mistrust was a conditioned response, learned from their interactions with one another in the classroom context, perhaps from the home environment, or even from society at large.

Perhaps even the influence of the classroom teacher, albeit unintentionally, could have contributed to a sense of suspicion and mistrust within the classroom. For example, through the planned learning and teaching, the teacher could have been setting up situations of competition, or through facetious or cynical replies to the children's comments in discussion. Equally, their response may have been due to my own presence among them.

Among the Year 3 children from the inner city school, this space could also have been characterized by discomfort. When invited to speak about what really mattered to them, an awkward silence seemed to descend upon the group. Several of the children appeared to be physically uncomfortable. They fidgeted, they squirmed, they avoided eye contact with one another; one child began tapping his pencil, almost as a nervous response to the uncomfortable space in which he found himself. It appeared that the children themselves were suspicious of this space. These children had come from classrooms that, as I had observed, seemed to be filled with constant noise. These spaces were busy spaces. However, they now found themselves in a space that was uncomfortably quiet, and in which they were being invited to consider something to which they had possibly never given a lot of thought. These particular children, it seemed, were not used to spaces characterized by stillness and silence. The space of uncomfortableness perhaps led them to feel vulnerable in the face of ultimate questions of meaning and value. In the classroom space, these children may have felt at home. However, in this space, they were left feeling disempowered by concepts about which they had previously spoken little, and about which they may not have possessed a language to convey their thoughts.

In this space, these children appeared self conscious. They seemed afraid to speak – to say 'the wrong thing' in front of their peers for fear of the reaction they might receive from them. They chose their words carefully so that their dialogue would be in keeping with a persona that would have been deemed acceptable within their social peer group. They concealed much of their genuine values behind a façade of materialism and trivializing. This appeared to be a means by which the children were able to cope with the space in which they found themselves. It seemed to work. Among the Year 5 children in the inner city school, each other's trivializing and materialistic comments were largely met with further smiling, giggling and the 'making light' of issues. Their chorused singing of a song from a recent episode of a popular television series was perhaps indicative of this, and epitomized the extent of their trivializing. It was their way of coping in this space of uncomfortableness, suspicion and mistrust.

At the same time, the space in which these children found themselves was one of ambiguity. While this space was one of mistrust, suspicion and uncomfortableness, it was also experienced by the children, in some instances, as a space of searching and of striving to articulate something of that which did indeed really matter to themselves – spiritual questing – as was evidenced in the previous chapter. Although the children were fearful of the reactions of their peers, and seemed to operate almost solely from their personas, on those instances when ultimate values were discussed, the children seemed to indicate a genuine searching for connectedness with Other. In this space, the children seemed to be receiving a mixed message. The message seemed to indicate that it was acceptable to search, to reveal something of the spiritual, of that which really mattered, but not too much! Hence, the space was to some extent ambiguous. It was perhaps little wonder that in some instances the children seemed reluctant to say anything at all. Perhaps they were searching for clues as to what to reveal, or as to what should remain concealed. The ambiguous nature of the space in which they found themselves may at times have rendered these children literally speechless, thereby inhibiting their expression of spirituality. Perhaps they questioned whether they were to act from their persona or from their shadow. The result was that a little of both may have occurred.

A time of shifting perceptions

The time in which the children were living was (and continues to be) one that has been described as shifting in terms of the ways in which people generally perceive, understand and make sense of their lives and the world. Such a shift can be conceived of in terms of a movement away from the certainty that perhaps was once characteristic of a classical worldview towards one in which there is a growing understanding that people themselves can define or construct their own understandings of reality from within their own particular life contexts (Horell 2003). In the classical worldview there was considered to be an objective reality that could be recognized with a significant degree of clarity. However, the present temporal horizon, marked by postmodernity, has seen a shift away from such an understanding. It is characterized by a multiplicity of meanings and realities for people, depending upon how these are created by individuals within the particularities of their own life contexts. There is no one objective reality.

It could be understood that the multiplicity of meanings indicative of the children's temporal milieu literally rendered them speechless when confronted with issues of meaning and value. With no single objective reality to cling to, the children initially remained silent as they attempted to question what is was that mattered most to them. This was particularly evident among the Year 3 children from the inner city school. The silence that prevailed was not a tranquil stillness. It was restless and awkward. They filled this silence with the distraction of movement and trivia and were unable to engage with issues of deeper meaning. Rather, these were continually repressed because the children were unskilled in engaging in moments of silence. In the lived time in which these children found themselves, appropriate moments of silence, solitude and stillness were absent and certainly, they are requirements for the process of discernment of what is of ultimate importance and value. Consequently, the children did not possess the necessary skills to engage in such moments of discernment.

This temporal milieu also gave rise to trivializing in terms of a manifestation of a loss of feeling and meaning. This could be seen particularly in the response of Ali in Year 3 from the inner city school to that which really mattered. He shrugged his shoulders. 'Nothing... I can't think of anything that is important to me,' he had replied. In this particular statement Ali was perhaps questioning whether it was really worth trying to make sense of life or the world. In the face of ambiguity and uncertainty it somehow seemed easier, or less bothersome to trivialize about issues of meaning and value. Perhaps also Ali's statement in some way reflected his minimal expectations in relation to those things that may have really mattered to him. Such negligible and token expectations were summed up in his view that nothing really mattered to him any more. This loss of meaning and feeling was also evident among the Year 5 children in the inner city school. It became apparent in their facetious comments, made both to one another and to myself. It could also be seen in the way they were quick to snigger at the responses made by their peers in relation to that which really mattered. It appeared that many of these children too had adopted the view that very little really mattered any more.

In a Nutshell

This chapter has examined two particular factors which seemed to inhibit the children's expression of their spirituality – material pursuit and trivializing.

Material pursuit

- entails a preference to relate to the material rather than to Other in community. It promotes a sense of disconnection with Other

- it involves a reliance upon the superficial self and that which might satisfy the ego

- becomes evident in a late capitalist consumer culture, in which society affirms children in material excess but ignores their basic spiritual needs

- manifests in a dangerous, yet enticing space full of consumer possibilities.

Trivializing

- entails the masking of inner feelings and values by creating a façade of complacency

- occurs when one acts solely through a persona of complacency and superficiality, in which issues of meaning and value are relegated to the shadow, where they are suppressed by the persona

- manifests in a space where mistrust, suspicion and ambiguity abound

- is present in a time characterized by a multiplicity of meanings, the absence of stillness, solitude and silence and, in some instances, a loss of feeling and meaning.

Some Guidelines for Counteracting these Factors

Creation of spaces which foster trust, respect and safety rather than mistrust and suspicion

- In the home such spaces can be encouraged by openness and honesty between parents and children. Placing trust in children indicates that adults value and affirm them. If the trust is broken, speak respectfully with each other to resolve the issue so that trust can be re-established.

- In the classroom these spaces can be encouraged by trust-building exercises. British educator Sue Phillips speaks about working with students in circles built on mutual trust and respect, where students are taught and can practise interpersonal skills through games and exercises (Phillips 2006). American educator Rachel Kessler, whose work was referred to in the previous chapter, suggests such spaces can be achieved through the incorporation of 'gateways to the soul' (Kessler 2000). For example, the first of Kessler's gateways – the yearning for deep connection – could be drawn on as a means by which to develop and foster relationships between students (and the teacher) that are caring, and in which students are able to feel a sense of connectedness to Other.

Addressing the consumerist temporal reality

- At home, try to affirm the value of simplicity. This is a challenge in Western society, but nonetheless, one that needs to be met. There is a saying: 'Live simply so that others can simply live'. Where possible, avoid unnecessary material excess. Show children that we, as adults, value our relationships with people rather than material excess.

- Spending time with children should not equate with spending money on them. Palmer (2007) affirms this principle, and has much practical advice to support parents in putting this into practice, for example, by relaxing and spending time in their children's company, sharing a hobby or interest with them, or by playing games (e.g. board games, outdoor kick abouts) to name but a few.

- In the classroom, education in relation to the concept of consumerism – both its constructive and damaging influences – can be addressed through several curriculum areas including English, studies of society and the environment, as well as through the arts, and religious education.

- Critique advertisements which promote materialism, and which try to entice people into spending money unnecessarily and excessively.

Enabling the shadow to emerge

- When issues of meaning and value arise at home, appropriately challenge children about their creation of meaning. This may enable the shadow to emerge and to challenge their persona.

- In the classroom, the use of moral dilemmas in the curriculum may be an effective means of enabling students' shadows to emerge and to challenge their personas. Religious education provides an immediate entry point for this to occur, but other areas of the curriculum, such as English and personal development, may equally provide opportunities for the inclusion of moral dilemmas.

Establishing opportunities for stillness, silence and solitude

In many instances, stillness, silence and solitude do not exist in the lived experiences of children. Yet these are essential for the consideration of issues of deeper meaning.

- At home, set aside quiet time, when the television is turned off and when ipods and other listening devices are put away. This need not be for excessively long periods, but is an effective means by which to build silence into daily routine.

- As a family, or even individually, take a leisurely stroll through the local park, or some other quiet space.

- In the classroom, plan activities in which to teach and practise the skills of stillness and silence. These are skills which many students do not have, and so need to be taught and practised. Guided meditation, or visualization activities are possible ways of skilling students in these areas. Jenny Garth's books *Starbright* and *Earthlight*, referred to in Chapter 6, are good resources that can be drawn upon to enable students to practise stillness, silence and solitude.

- Make use of quiet spaces around the school or establish such areas by, for example, drawing on existing gardens or grassed areas, designating quiet rooms in which children read, draw, or relax on comfortable chairs.

CHAPTER 10

Nurturing the Spiritual Dimension of Children's Lives

The research presented in this book sought to explore the spiritual dimension of children's lives by identifying characteristics of their spirituality. In identifying these characteristics, it has been my hope that these may provide an indication as to what adults who engage with children – in particular parents and teachers – might look for and be alert to in recognizing when children may be expressing their spirituality. In being able to recognize it, they may then be in a position to actively nurture the spirituality of the children with whom they engage. From the many short examples of hermeneutic phenomenological writing taken from my reflective journal and presented in the previous chapters, it became clear that the children who participated in my investigation did in fact possess a rich spiritual dimension to their lives. There were four characteristics of their spirituality which were identified, and which attest to the existence of this dimension – the felt sense, integrating awareness, weaving the threads of meaning, and spiritual questing. As well, two factors which appeared to inhibit the children's expression of their spirituality were also identified and discussed. These were termed as material pursuit and trivializing.

In this final chapter, I want to do three things. First, I want to suggest some general recommendations for nurturing the spiritual dimension of children's lives. In each of the preceding chapters in Part 2 of this book, I have offered some guidelines for nurturing each of the particular characteristics of children's spirituality, and for counteracting the inhibiting factors. In this chapter, I will bring these together more generally under the headings of space, time, body and relationships (cf. van Manen 1990). Second, I want to briefly outline a possible pedagogical framework for nurturing spirituality in the classroom context. This is important for teachers who take seriously the education of the whole child – cognitively, emotionally and spiritually. Third, I will briefly address some continuing issues which may remain a concern for some readers, particularly the notion of relativism as it pertains to the characteristics of weaving the threads of meaning and spiritual questing.

Space

One of the key aspects which has been brought to the fore in reflecting on each of the characteristics of children's spirituality is the notion of space, and specifically, the types of spaces and environments which nurture spirituality. For the most part, adults have a responsibility in furnishing and maintaining such spaces, although as I shall discuss shortly, children can also play a role in creating them. The reflections on weaving the threads of meaning and spiritual questing place a clear onus on adults in terms of the creation of appropriate spaces for nurturing spirituality. Weaving the threads of meaning pertains to children drawing on their own sense of wonder in creating their worldview. They appear to do this by entering the spaces between the various frameworks of meaning to select eclectically those elements from each which have meaning for them, and weaving these into a personal framework of meaning. There are two 'levels' of space here. First, there is the space in which children feel free to weave together a worldview. That is, the classroom space, or the family/home space. Adults have a clear responsibility here. Is the space an established one which enables and encourages children to engage in the act of meaning-making? Is it a space characterized by mutual trust, respect and open enquiry? Is it a space of safety? Children living in the postmodern world, in which there is no one frame of reference for anything, will seek out and create their own worldviews regardless of the wishes of adults. However, some of the frameworks of meaning in which children seek meaning are ambiguous, and potentially dangerous. For example, the media – and in particular television – is a valuable and entertaining framework, yet at the same time it could be a precarious one since it presents a virtual frame of reality. Programmes classified as 'reality TV' such as the *Big Brother* series, *Survival*, and the like, present a worldview which, strangely enough, is not necessarily akin to reality! It is nonsensical to shelter children from these, since they are generally screened before children's bedtimes and, in being both astute and ingenious, children will find ways of watching them. The role of the adult then becomes one of a guide as children weave together their worldview. Does the family space, or indeed the classroom space act as a space of guidance? Does it act as space which respects and trusts children in their ability to weave the threads of meaning, while at the same time, providing the necessary guidance and scaffolding to support them in this task?

Second, there are the spaces between the frameworks of meaning. These are enticing spaces. They are spaces full of opportunity and choice. While adults have little control over such spaces, they can act as responsible partners (Ota 2001) in accompanying children in entering the spaces between the many frameworks of meaning. Again, the importance of the adult as guide here is pertinent. Adults cannot weave their own framework together for children, as much as many adults would possibly like to. This is a task that children need to accomplish on their own. However, adults can and should act as guides, or responsible partners in this process. They can do this by accompanying children in the spaces between the frameworks of meaning, mentoring and offering support where necessary, and taking a more passive role as required.

The notion of space is also important in considering spiritual questing. In my research, this space was both a space of possibility and ambiguity. It was a space of possibility in so far as spiritual questing involves those who engage with it in a search for authentic ways of being in the world and of relating with Other. Yet at times, the space can also act so as to stifle any questing that might occur, particularly when it is characterized by suspicion, mistrust, and ambiguity. Again, adults can play an important role in creating the types of spaces that enable spiritual questing to occur.

In contemplating issues of meaning and value, which are at the heart of spiritual questing, appropriate spaces would also be characterized by silence. Silence, stillness and reflection are qualities that are often absent from children's lives. In contemporary classrooms, the hustle and bustle of daily activity is given precedence. In homes, the intrusion of television, computers, iPods, telephones and the like often abound in preference to silence. In Western culture, people are uncomfortable with the quiet, and they try to fill the silence with noise of one kind or another. For children, silence, stillness and reflection are skills that need to be taught and practised both in the classroom and at home. It is impossible to address issues of meaning and value without some mastery of these skills. Adults need to ensure that the spaces provided for spiritual questing allow opportunities for silence, stillness and reflection. In classrooms, such skills need to be explicitly taught and practised. In other words, they need to be programmed into the curriculum. At home, spaces need to be provided that are free from the intrusion of electronic media – for at least some of the time.

However, children too are able to create appropriate spaces for nurturing their own spirituality, and should be allowed to do so. This is particularly evident in relation to integrating awareness. This may require, in some instances, the parent or teacher to be absent from the spaces that children create for themselves if their spirituality is to be genuinely expressed. The chapter exploring integrating awareness illustrated how some elements of the children's conversation may not have emerged in the ordinary classroom context in which a teacher is present and monitoring the dialogue. While teachers and parents would not necessarily wish to encourage conversation of a potentially inappropriate nature, the spaces children create for their own nurturing of spirituality need to be envisaged by them as safe and confidential. This requires wisdom, sensitivity and trust on the part of the adult to be able to remove her or himself from these spaces when deemed necessary.

Time

Another key aspect which has been brought to the fore in reflecting on each of the characteristics of children's spirituality is time. In relation to the felt sense, time to engage in the present moment of experience is a necessary requirement. In Western culture, this is a skill which most adults seem to have lost – and it is difficult to reclaim. If the felt sense is to be nurtured, then parents and educators must enable opportunities for children to engage in the here and now of their experiences. In the present classroom climate of Western education, many would argue that it is a brave teacher who puts the curriculum on hold to enable children to simply sit, to be, and to engage in the present moment. It is perceived as 'doing nothing' and is considered to be time wasting. Yet brave teachers are required! It is a wise teacher indeed who perceives one's bodily wisdom as a primal way of knowing, and who is willing to draw upon this and build it into the curriculum. Perhaps what are needed are opportunities for both personal and professional learning, for teachers and for those who devise school curricula at the systems level in terms of recognizing the value of the felt sense.

Similarly, it takes a wise parent to recognize that when, for example, her or his child is clutching at a small rock, or is captivated by running fingers through the mud (usually when time for doing so is in short supply!), that the child may be expressing her or his spirituality, and allow time for the child to engage in the present moment. Often such experiences and opportunities cannot be planned. Those things which attract the attention of children are not the things we as adults imagine. Therefore, whether at home or in the classroom, adults need to be prepared to seize the opportunities when and if they arise in allowing children to engage in the here and now of time.

On another level, the present time in which we live, described by those in philosophical circles as postmodern, abounds with opportunities for children to weave the threads of meaning and to spiritually quest. It is a time which actively encourages children to search in all sorts of places for a sense of life's meaning and purpose, and to seek out authentic ways of connecting with Self and Other. In postmodernity, there is no one absolute framework of meaning or one narrative that captures reality. These are considered to be individually constructed by people as they engage with the world and make sense of their lives. Some people argue ferociously against this, claiming that it results in relativism, a claim that suggests it is impossible to judge between different individual values, patterns of behaviour, and competing truth claims. All is considered to be relative, and no one way of seeing the world, of behaving, or making decisions is any better or worse than another (the issue of relativism will be addressed later in this chapter). As frightening as this may seem to some, adults need to take seriously the present temporal milieu. This is especially so when the worldviews and questing of children lies beyond what once may have been considered to be the accepted classical, or foundational worldview. In essence, adults need to dialogue with the immediate temporal horizon.

However, the present milieu can also act in a destructive way on children's spirituality. In considering material pursuit, the present time is marked by a consumerist milieu in which children can be tempted to place their value in their spending power rather than in relationships with others. In some instances, parents may have inadvertently fuelled this destructive factor. In a competitive consumer society, Palmer (2007) notes the ease with which spending money on children can be equated with love. Children often come home not to parental time and attention, but to an array of expensive gadgets and appliances in the form of televisions, PlayStations, radios, iPods, MP3 players, computer games, expensive designer label clothes, and the like. Such overspending on the part of adults may be the result of guilt, over protectiveness, anxiety or a belief that such acquisitions equate with contentment. Whatever the case, parents may themselves have become victims of the temporal consumerist milieu and, unintentionally, contribute to a factor which can be destructive of their children's spirituality.

While this may be challenging, the clear message here is for parents to provide a balance. Spending money on children to provide them with gifts and small luxuries is understandable, but not to the extent that it becomes a destructive influence on their spirituality. The more parents unnecessarily spend on their children, the more the children themselves may come to place a value on consumerism. A balance needs to be sought. Where possible, parents need to avoid unnecessary material excess. Show children that, as parents, you value your relationships with people and with them, rather than material excess.

Body

Corporeality is a primal way of knowing, and the felt sense attests to bodily awareness as natural way of knowing. Importantly, Gendlin (1981) reiterates an holistic understanding of the body as including both the mental and physical capacities of the person. His understanding encompasses both body and mind. So, when children attend to their felt sense, they draw upon the wisdom of their bodies in an holistic sense, which includes both the physical and mental realms.

The implications for classroom practice here are clear. Sensorial, tactile, 'hands-on' activities must be an integral part of the curriculum if this feature of children's spirituality is to be nurtured. In kindergartens and classrooms which follow the philosophy of Maria Montessori, such activities and experiences are commonplace, and have a privileged place in the curriculum. However, in mainstream schooling, the use of tactile material is often phased out quite early – in some instances, by the end of the first year of formal schooling. In the early years classrooms of faith schools, and in some Sunday School settings, the religious education programme sometimes draws on Montessorian principles through Godly Play (Berryman 1991), or The Catechesis of the Good Shepherd (Cavalletti 1983). I have critiqued previously these approaches for their contributions to nurturing children's spirituality (Hyde 2004b). These approaches to catechesis utilize tactile experiences, and so can make a positive contribution to nurturing children's spirituality. However, these approaches are limited to faith schools and related contexts. The broader curriculum of the mainstream primary school classroom can and should use sensorial, 'hands-on' activities in a variety of subject areas. In a system of schooling which favours the intellect, and in which even young children are initiated into the abstractions of written language and numeracy by the end of their first year of formal schooling, giving a privileged place to tactile activity as a natural way of knowing may be challenging. Early childhood educators have long advocated for such experiences, and unless the voice of their expertise is heeded and taken seriously, it will be difficult to nurture the felt sense as a characteristic of children's spirituality in the classroom contexts of mainstream schooling.

At home, it is important for parents to recognize also that bodily awareness is a natural way of knowing. Children playing in the sand, making mud pies, rolling in the grass, finger painting, and the like are engaged in tactile activities which may enable them to draw upon the wisdom of their bodies as a natural way of knowing, albeit a sometimes messy way of knowing. Even very young children playing with their food in the high chair could be an example of bodily knowing. When children are able to engage in these types of activities for extended periods of time (playing with food being a possible exception), they may be attending to their felt sense, and therefore may be expressing their spirituality. Parents would need to recognize this potential feature of their child's spirituality and be prepared to nurture it by allowing them to engage with the particular activity, and if appropriate, even to join in the activity. Playing with a child in the sand, helping to make a mud pie, and rolling in the grass or through the autumn leaves with a child may even lead a parent to reclaim their body as a natural source of knowledge, and rediscover that particular feature of their own spirituality.

In relation to integrating awareness, it was the initial engagement in tactile activity which prepared the ground for an emerging level of consciousness to arise. While not every sensory activity which is undertaken by children will lead to an integrating of awareness (and nor would teachers or parents necessarily want them to), bodily awareness in relation to particular 'hands-on' activities may, given the right ambiance, enable children the opportunity to integrate an emerging wave of consciousness with their initial physical awareness. That is, opportunities both in the classroom as well as in the home may be provided for children to develop their spirituality in this particular way.

Relationships

Underpinning all of the characteristics of children's spirituality is the notion of relationality. The centrality of relationality was highlighted in Chapter 2, and it has been a pivotal element in the reflections upon each of the characteristics of children's spirituality. In some instances, particularly in relation to the felt sense and integrating awareness, the relationship experienced between Self and that which was other than Self was so connected that it resulted in a sense of unity, albeit for a short time. In relation to weaving the threads of meaning and spiritual questing, relationality is also pertinent. For example, Michelle from the rural school community used her sense of wonder to weave together a worldview that would enable her to remain connected – even unified – with her deceased older sister, Kim. This was a heightened sense of kinship which extended across the boundaries of the living and dead.

In their active seeking and spiritual questing, the children sought authentic ways of connecting with Self and Other, for example through family, through the larger themes of life, and through acts of altruism. Those things that really mattered to the children were, largely and in relation to spiritual questing, their sense of relationality with others, and in some instances, with God.

Again, there are clear implications for adults who engage with children in various capacities. The centrality of relationships is paramount. In the classroom, teachers need to support and nurture the children's relationships with each other and with themselves as educators. Focusing on the sense of relationships between people helps children to develop a sense of empathy and compassion for Other. Both empathy and compassion are qualities that many consider to be lacking in Western culture. Yet for children who develop relationships readily with Other, this can be exhibited quite naturally. Hay and Nye (2006) would argue that this is because these qualities underlie the altruistic impulse of biological relational consciousness. They are traits which are 'hard-wired' into the human person.

When relationships do break down – as they can and do – parents and teachers need to put in place processes for restoring the sense of connectedness. Educators such as Kessler (2000) and Phillips (2006) both suggest ways in which relationships might be nurtured, and processes for mending them when they do break down. Palmer (2007) highlights the importance of communication at home between siblings and between parents and their children. While children's squabbling and fighting can be quite hurtful to one another, anyone who has worked with children, or who has parented children, will be quick to point to the relative ease with which they seem to be able to forgive and to mend their relationships with each other, particularly if they are given the encouragement and support to do so.

A Possible Pedagogical Model for the Classroom

In this section of the chapter, I want to focus on the primary classroom, and briefly offer one pedagogical model which I have been developing (see Hyde 2004c, 2006b), and which could be used for nurturing spirituality in the context of the primary classroom.[20] Good learning and teaching has reiterated that, not only are each of these dimensions interrelated, but also that students do not learn solely in any one dimension, and that learning involves the engagement of a combination of different dimensions, both cognitive and non-cognitive. Those familiar with learning and teaching models generally will recognize two of the dimensions in which children learn; however, the third area of my model – the spiritual dimension – is often not articulated by teachers, or it is ignored altogether. With this in mind, I will briefly outline each dimension of learning in my model and provide practical examples of the types of activities which may engage children in that particular dimension of learning.

The first is the cognitive dimension and is concerned with the acquisition of knowledge, skills and understandings in relation to the content of particular subject areas. Benjamin Bloom and his colleagues were among the first to explicitly bring this dimension of learning to the fore through the development of their taxonomy for educational objectives in this dimension (Bloom 1956). In a curriculum topic which has a focus on, for example, life cycles, the cognitive content could include an exploration of the life cycles of butterflies, frogs, and other animals, that is, learning specific information about these creatures, and about the life cycles of these creatures. It could also include developing, refining and mastering the skills of recording information, taking notes, making predictions, testing hypotheses, and the like.

In Western education, the cognitive dimension is the sphere in which learning is commonly addressed. It is often given precedence over other dimensions of learning. This can be a concern in primary classrooms because the principles of developmentally appropriate practice maintain that all domains of development in children are interrelated and that development in one domain influences and is influenced by development in the other realms. If the focus remains in one area, for example, the cognitive, then the other areas are understood to be violated (Bredekamp and Copple 1997). Therefore learning must go beyond the cognitive dimension to include an engagement of the non-cognitive realms.

There are two particular non-cognitive realms that form part of the pedagogical model I wish to offer. The first is the emotional or affective dimension. This is concerned with the feelings, emotions and reactions of learners to the content of particular subject matter. The affective dimension in the learning process has often been ignored by cognitive theorists,[21] yet the role of the emotions in the intellectual performance and in the life of the student has been argued to be an important factor in the learning process (de Souza 2004, 2006). In a curriculum topic which has a focus on, for example, life cycles, the affective dimension could be addressed through an exploration of children's feeling in relation to the different seasons of the year, life, grief and loss, and the like. These feelings and reactions would impact upon how and what the children learn. There is much evidence to suggest that the affective dimension complements learning in the cognitive realm. Therefore, its inclusion in the learning process ought not be neglected.

The second non-cognitive realm is the spiritual dimension. In drawing upon the discussion of spirituality presented in this book, the spiritual dimension concerns the sense of relationality, connectedness, and in some instances, the sense of unity children experience with Self, and with everything Other than Self. It is in this dimension that attention could be paid to nurturing each of the particular characteristics of children's spirituality that have been outlined in this book. For example, in the topic of life cycles, opportunities for nurturing the felt sense could be planned through activities which involve children in nature walks, where they may physically come into contact with the cycles of nature – feeling the elements of a particular season (the cold of winter, the warmth of the sun), collecting cocoons, tadpoles and the like. Opportunities for weaving the threads of meaning could include an exploration of picture story books which deal with the themes of living and dying, such as Margaret Wild's *Toby*. Opportunities for spiritual questing could include an exploration of what really matters to children in nature, in life, in their relationships with other people.

In general terms, the spiritual dimension is essential for the effective functioning of both cognition and affect (see de Souza 2006; Zohar and Marshall 2000). Neither cognition nor the emotions operate separately. Zohar and Marshall in fact argue that the spiritual dimension integrates both a person's intellect and their emotions. Therefore in effective learning and teaching, all three dimensions need to be addressed and balanced within the curriculum.

The pedagogical model I have developed then comprises three moments – the cognitive, the affective and the spiritual. Any one of these three moments could provide an entry point to a particular topic. Further, it is possible to devise activities which effectually address all three dimensions.[22] Nor does the model demand any one specific learning and teaching methodology. It has its origin in a spiral, rather than a linear framework of learning (see Wright 2000). In a spiral framework, the learner may continually circle around a particular theme or topic, beginning with, for example, the spiritual and moving then to the affective and cognitive dimensions, before returning to the spiritual with new insights and then moving again to the other dimensions. In this way, the learner is continually building new insights and understandings.

Continuing Issues

Some readers may have reached this point and still have some lingering concerns, particularly in relation to two of the characteristics of children's spirituality that I have presented, namely weaving the threads of meaning and spiritual questing. The specific concern with these two characteristics, as I have discerned from some critics of my work, centres on the notion of relativism. I would like briefly to address the notion of relativism in relation to weaving the threads of meaning and spiritual questing.

Relativism

Relativism arises from within the postmodern context which claims that there is no one overarching theory or grand narrative that explains the world from an objective viewpoint. There are only individual narratives based on the particular perspectives which have been constructed by individuals within their own cultural and historical life contexts. Many would argue that this leads to relativism, which maintains that it is therefore impossible to judge objectively between different individual values, behaviour patterns, and competing truth claims, since these are all culturally and historically bound (Engebretson 2007). Everything is relative, and no one way of seeing the world, judging truth claims, or making decisions is any better or worse than another. Taken to its extreme, Hay and Nye (2006) note that relativism is the view that there is no possibility of objective knowledge, and thus, all supposed knowledge is really little more than a culturally constructed fiction.

Some could argue that characteristics of children's spirituality like weaving the threads of meaning and spiritual questing actually promote and encourage relativism. In a sense this may be true. Children do actively create their own worldview based on their choosing from among the different frameworks of meaning. And, they do search for a sense of life's meaning and purpose in places to which they feel drawn. Certainly, and as has been discussed, postmodernity encourages this type of searching. In this sense, the children in my research were products of their time in culture and history. However, the weaving and questing of the children who took part in my study appeared to be an intentional act of meaning-making. That is, the worldviews they were in the process of weaving were not necessarily viewed by themselves as being relative. For the children, they held meaning. It did not appear to be a case of consumer choice, or 'whateverism' (Hughes 2007). Indeed they chose, but their choice appeared to be based not on consumer options, but rather on that which held meaning for them. Similarly, the spiritual questing undertaken by them appeared not to be a matter of choosing this or that particular value, but a genuine searching for that which provided a means of relating authentically with Other. Their weaving and searching was not viewed necessarily as making a selection from among many options, with each being no better or worse than the others. Rather, it was a deliberate act of locating that which held meaning, and that which enabled them to relate meaningfully to Other. I am not saying that children and young people always act with such intentionality. There is plenty of research to suggest the contrary. However, the findings of my study do challenge the view proprosed by some that children and young people have a consumer sense of spirituality – that one sense of the spiritual is as good as any other, and that it can be discarded when it loses its usefulness.

In reflecting upon the interrelatedness of thinking and feeling, the work of Bowker (2005) supports my counter claim to relativism on the part of the children in my study. Bowker affirms the realization that knowing is a function of the whole person, that is, a function of the whole thinking/feeling body. Rationality and emotion are intricately intertwined, and both are drawn upon by people when they attempt to make sense of the world in which they live. Bowker points out that people have hard-wired rational/emotional responses to different aspects of reality. In other words, there is a biological basis to the ways in which people respond to and make sense of their world. This may counter the relativist claim that people can make whatever world they so like through social construction. Their biological predispositions ensure that subjectivity is not arbitrary. Therefore, when children weave together the threads of meaning, or are engaged in spiritual questing, the subjectivity of what they choose is not relative or arbitrary, but is based rather upon their intertwined functions of thinking and feeling. Their biology ensures that their subjectivity in relation to these activities is not arbitrary. This has quite overt parallels with the notion that spirituality has a biological basis (Hardy 1966; Hay and Nye 2006; Newberg et al. 2001), and that the qualities that have been favoured in the evolutionary process of human beings may come to the fore in activities like weaving the threads of meaning, or spiritual questing. Certainly, the children's weaving and questing was subjective. But it was not arbitrary.

Conclusion

The findings of my study affirm the fact that children clearly possess a rich spiritual dimension to their lives, which can be nurtured if those who spend time with them are alert to the features and characteristics of their spirituality. Each of the four characteristics identified in my investigation – the felt sense, integrating awareness, weaving the threads of meaning, and spiritual questing – can be detected and nurtured by parents, teachers, and others who engage with children in various capacities. The fact that I have identified four characteristics does not negate the fact that there are almost certainly others. Further research is needed to determine these, and to provide further tangible signs for adults to effectively enable them to nurture the spiritual dimension of children's lives.

Notes

Chapter One: Introduction

1   The vignettes described are drawn from numerous observations and anecdotes collected over time. They do not necessarily come from the body of research described in this book. The names of the children have been fictionalized.

Chapter Two: Mapping the Terrain

2   For an example of the diversity of understandings in relation to the term 'spirituality', see Beringer (2000) and Kohn (1996).

3   For a comprehensive treatment of the Christian mystical tradition, see Davis (2006).

4   For an overview of Aurobindo's philosophy, see also Maitra (1968).

5   See also Wilber (2000b).

6   I am indebted to the many discussions with my mentor and colleague, Dr Marian de Souza, for the development of this particular insight.

7   Some critics of my work argue that I am making a strong ontological claim here – that Other exists not just as a perception, but as reality. My own prejudice aside, not only do the writings of the Eastern and Western mystical traditions suggest and support this, but my claim also finds support from transpersonal psychology as well as from some neuro-scientific research, particularly that of Andrew Newberg and his colleagues.

Chapter 3: Research on the Spirituality of Childhood

8   For a detailed account of the notion of connectedness with family and community acting as a protective factor and a means by which to build resilience in the young, see Eckersley (2005).

Chapter 4: An Approach for Understanding the Expressions of Human Life

9   There are a growing number of investigations within the field of children's spirituality which have dispelled the notion of complete objectivity on the part of the researcher. Notable among these are the research of the Errickers and their colleagues, as well as that of Hay and Nye. See also Scott (2001).

10   For a detailed understanding of phenomenology and hermeneutics respectively, see Husserl (1976) and Heidegger (1980).

11   For an insightful exploration of the notion of spatiality, as well as the other lifeworld existentials, see Merleau-Ponty (1996, 2004).

Chapter 5: The Felt Sense

12   An earlier version of some material in this chapter has previously appeared in Hyde (2006b).

Chapter 6: Integrating Awareness

13   Although Wilber (2000a, b) uses 'self' with an initial lower case, it would seem that his use of the term 'self' refers to the individual's true Self. Hence, in discussing Wilber's Self system, I have used 'Self' with an initial capital, consistent with the understanding of Self outlined in Chapter 2.

Chapter 7: Weaving the Threads of Meaning

14   These are two popular television programmes shown in many Western countries. *Touched by an Angel* depicts three angels who intervene in the lives of people, while the host of *Crossing Over* is said to be able to communicate with the deceased loved ones of members of the studio audience who appear on that programme.

15   Michelle's epiphany of her deceased older sister, Kim, parallels with Hart's (2003) description of 'seeing the invisible' as a feature of children's spirituality.

16   For a clear and succinct description of modernity and postmodernity in relation to spirituality and young people, see Chapter 9 of Engebretson (2007).

Chapter 8: Spiritual Questing

17   Although Horell (2003) uses the term 'self' with an initial lower case, it would seem that his usage of this term reflects the notion of a person's true Self, and therefore reflects the understanding of Self which has been advocated throughout this book.

Chapter 9: Factors that Inhibit Spirituality

18 An earlier version of some material in this chapter has previously been published in Hyde (2006a).

19 In relation to the archetypes of persona and shadow, see also Tacey (2003).

Chapter 10: Nurturing the Spiritual Dimension of Children's Lives

20 The particular pedagogical model I have been developing has been influenced by Dr Marian de Souza, and I am indebted to her for her constant insight and encouragement.

21 One notable exception here would be the work of Krathwohl and his colleagues, who devised a taxonomy of educational objectives in the affective domain. See Krathwohl, Bloom and Masia (1964).

22 A number of my undergraduate students at the Australian Catholic University have been engaged in developing learning and teaching activities for particular religious education topics which address each of the three dimensions of learning.

Bibliography

Adams, K. (2001) 'God talks to me in my dreams: The occurrence and significance of children's dreams about God.' *International Journal of Children's Spirituality 6*, 1, 99–111.

Adams, K. (2003) 'Children's dreams: An exploration of Jung's concept of big dreams.' *International Journal of Children's Spirituality 8*, 2, 105–114.

Austin, J. (2000) 'Consciousness Evolves when Self Dissolves.' In J. Andresen and R. Forman (eds) *Cognitive Models and Spiritual Maps: Interdisciplinary Explorations of Religious Experience.* Thorverton, UK: Imprint Academic.

Berryman, J. (1999) *Godly Play, A Way of Religions Education.* San Francisco: Harper.

Berryman, J. (2001) 'The Nonverbal Nature of Spirituality and Religious Language.' In J. Erricker, C. Ota and C. Erricker (eds) *Spiritual Education. Cultural, Religious and Social Differences: New Perspectives for the 21st Century.* Brighton: Sussex Academic.

Beringer, A. (2000) 'In search of the sacred: A conceptual analysis of spirituality.' *Journal of Experiential Education,* Boulder, Winter, 157–167. Accessed 28 May 2001 at http://global.umi.com

Billington, R. (1997) *Understanding Eastern Philosophy.* London: Routledge.

Bloom, B. (ed.) (1956) *Taxonomy of Educational Objectives. The Classification of Educational Goals. Book 1: Cognitive Domain.* London: Longman.

Boyer, P. (1994) 'Cognitive Constraints on Cultural Representations: Natural Ontologies and Religious Ideas.' In L. Hirschfeld and S. Gelman (eds) *Mapping the Mind: Domain Specificity in Cognition and Culture.* Cambridge: Cambridge University Press.

Bowker, J. (2005) *The Sacred Neuron: Extraordinary Discoveries Linking Science and Religion.* London: JB Taurus.

Bredekamp, S. and Copple, C. (eds) *Developmentally Appropriate Practice in Early Childhood Programs.* Washington: National Association for the Education of Young Children.

Broadbent, J. (2004) 'Embodying the abstract: Enhancing children's spirituality through creative dance.' *International Journal of Children's Spirituality 9*, 1, 97–104.

Bryman, A. (2001) *Social Research Methods.* Oxford: Oxford University Press.

Carr, D. (1995) 'Towards a distinctive conception of spiritual education.' *Oxford Review of Education 21*, 1, 83–97.

Cavalletti, S. (1983) *The Religious Potential of the Child: The Description of an Experience with Children from Ages Three to Six.* New York, NY: Paulist Press.

Champagne, E. (2001) 'Listening to… Listening for…: A Theological Reflection on Spirituality in Early Childhood.' In J. Erricker, C. Ota and C. Erricker (eds) *Spiritual Education. Cultural, Religious and Social Differences: New Perspectives for the 21st Century.* Brighton: Sussex Academic.

Champagne, E. (2003) 'Being a child, a spiritual child.' *International Journal of Children's Spirituality 8*, 1, 43–53.

Chater, M. (2001) 'Children, Doorposts and Hearts: How Can and Should the Religious Traditions Respond to Spirituality in a Postmodern Setting?' In J. Erricker, C. Ota and C. Erricker (eds) *Spiritual Education. Cultural, Religious and Social Differences: New Perspectives for the 21st Century*. Brighton: Sussex Academic.

Coles, R. (1990) *The Spiritual Life of Children*. London: HarperCollins.

Cottingham, M. (2005) 'Developing spirituality through the use of literature in history education.' *International Journal of Children's Spirituality 10*, 1, 45–60.

Crawford, M. and Rossiter, G. (2003) 'Reasons for living: School education and young people's search for meaning, spirituality and identity.' *Journal of Religious Education 51*, 4, 2–12.

Crawford, M. and Rossiter, G. (2006) *Reasons for Living: Education and Young People's Search for Meaning, Identity and Spirituality*. Melbourne, Australia: Australian Council for Educational Research.

Creswell, J. (1998) *Qualitative Inquiry and Research Design: Choosing Among Five Traditions*. London: Sage.

Crotty, M. (1998) *The Foundations of Social Research: Meaning and Perspective in the Research Process*. Crows Nest, NSW: Allen and Unwin.

Csikszentmihalyi, M. (1975) *Beyond Boredom and Anxiety: Experiencing Flow in Work and Play*. San Francisco, CA: Jossey-Bass.

Csikszentmihalyi, M. (1990) *Flow: The Psychology of Optimal Experience*. New York, NY: HarperPerennial.

Davis, O. (2006) *God Within: The Mystical Tradition of Northern Europe*. London: Darton, Longman and Todd.

Del Prete, T. (2002) 'Being What We Are: Thomas Merton's Spirituality of Education.' In J. Miller and Y. Nakagawa (eds) *Nurturing Our Wholeness: Perspectives on Spirituality in Education*. Rutland, VT: Foundation for Educational Renewal.

de Souza, M. (2004) 'Teaching for effective learning in religious education: A discussion of the perceiving, thinking, feeling and intuitive elements in the learning process.' *Journal of Religious Education 52*, 3, 22–30.

de Souza, M. (2005) 'Engaging the mind, heart and soul of the student in religious education: Teaching for meaning and connection.' *Journal of Religious Education 53*, 4, 40–47.

de Souza, M. (2006) 'Rediscovering the Spiritual Dimension in Education: Promoting a Sense of Self and Place, Meaning and Purpose in Learning.' In M. de Souza, K. Engebreston, G. Durka, R. Jackson and A. McGrady (eds) *International Handbook of the Religious, Moral and Spiritual Dimensions in Education*. Dordrecht, The Netherlands: Springer.

Donaldson, M. (1992) *Human Minds: An Exploration*. London: Allen Lane/Penguin Press.

Drane, J. (2000) *The McDonaldization of the Church: Spirituality, Creativity, and the Future of the Church*. London: Darton, Longman and Todd.

Durham, W. (1991) *Co-evolution: Genes, Culture, and Human Diversity*. Stanford, CA: Stanford University Press.

Eaude, T. (2003) 'Shining lights in unexpected corners: New angles on young children's spiritual development.' *International Journal of Children's Spirituality 8*, 2, 151–162.

Eckersley, R. (1998) *Casualties of Change – The Predicament of Youth in Australia.* Canberra, ACT: Commission for the Future.

Eckersley, R. (2005) *Well and Good: Morality, Meaning and Happiness* (2nd edn). Melbourne: Text Publishing.

Emmons, R. (1999) *The Psychology of Ultimate Concerns: Motivation and Spirituality in Personality.* New York, NY: Guilford.

Emmons, R. (2000) 'Is spirituality an intelligence? Motivation, cognition, and the psychology of ultimate concern.' *International Journal for the Psychology of Religion 10,* 1, 3–26.

Engebretson, K. (2007) *Connecting: Teenage Boys, Spirituality and Religious Education.* Strathfield, NSW: St. Paul's.

Erricker, C. (2001) 'Shall we dance? Authority, representation, and voice: The place of spirituality in religious education.' *Religious Education 96,* 1, 20–35.

Erricker, C. and Erricker, J. (1996) 'Where Angels Fear to Tread: Discovering Children's Spirituality.' In R. Best (ed.) *Education, Spirituality and the Whole Child.* London: Cassell.

Erricker, C., Erricker, J., Sullivan, D., Ota, C. and Fletcher, M. (1997) *The Education of the Whole Child.* London: Cassell.

Finley, J. (2003) *Merton's Place of Nowhere.* Notre Dame, IN: Ave Maria Press.

Fontana, D. (2003) *Psychology, Religion and Spirituality.* Oxford: BPS Blackwell.

Gadamer, H. (1989) *Truth and Method* (trans. J. Weinsheimer and D. Marshall). London: Sheed and Ward.

Garth, M. (1992) *Starbright: Meditations for Children* (2nd edn). North Blackburn, VIC: CollinsDove.

Garth, M. (1997) *Earthlight: New Meditations for Children.* Pymble, NSW: HarperCollins.

Gendlin, E. (1962) *Experiencing and the Creation of Meaning.* Chicago, IL: Free Press of Glencoe.

Gendlin, E. (1981) *Focusing* (2nd edn). New York, NY: Bantam.

Griffiths, B. (1984) *Christ in India: Essays Towards a Hindu-Christian Dialogue.* Springfield, IL: Templegate.

Griffiths, B. (2002) *Return to the Centre.* Springfield, IL: Templegate.

Groome, T. (1998) *Educating for Life: A Spiritual Vision for every Teacher and Parent.* New York, NY: Crossroads.

Halstead, J. and Waite, S. (2001) 'Nurturing the spiritual in children's sexual development.' *International Journal of Children's Spirituality 6,* 2, 185–206.

Hampshire County Council (2006) *Living Difference – The Primary Handbook.* Hampshire: Hampshire County Council.

Hardy, A. (1966) *The Divine Flame: An Essay towards a Natural History of Religion.* London: Collins.

Hart, T. (2003) *The Secret Spiritual World of Children.* Makawao, HI: Inner Ocean.

Hay, D. (2001) 'Spirituality versus Individualism: The Challenge of Relational Consciousness.' In J. Erricker, C. Ota and C. Erricker (eds) *Spiritual Education. Cultural, Religious and Social Differences: New Perspectives for the 21st Century.* Brighton: Sussex Academic.

Hay, D. and Nye, R. (2006) *The Spirit of the Child* (rev. edn). London: Jessica Kingsley Publishers.

Heidegger, M. (1980) *Being and Time* (trans. J. Macquarrie and E. Robinson). Oxford: Blackwell.

Heller, D. (1986) *The Children's God*. Chicago, IL: The University of Chicago Press.

Helminiak, D. (1996) *The Human Core of Spirituality: Mind as Psyche and Spirit*. Albany, NY: State University of New York Press.

Hicks, R. and Hicks, K. (1999) *Boomers, Xers, and Other Strangers: Understanding the Generational Differences that Divide Us*. Wheaton, IL: Tyndale.

Hill, B., Knitter, P. and Madges, W. (2002) *Faith, Religion and Theology: A Contemporary Introduction* (rev edn). Mystic, CT: Twenty-Third Publications.

Hirschfeld, L. and Gelman, S. (1994) 'Towards a Topography of Mind: An Introduction to Domain Specificity.' In L. Hirschfeld and S. Gelman (eds) *Mapping the Mind: Domain Specificity in Cognition and Culture*. Cambridge: Cambridge University Press.

Horell, H. (2003) 'Cultural Postmodernity and Christian Faith Formation.' In T. Groome and H. Horell (eds) *Horizons and Hopes: The Future of Religious Education*. New York, NY: Paulist Press.

Horell, H. (2004) 'Fostering hope: Christian religious education in a postmodern age.' *Religious Education 99*, 1, 5–22.

Howe, N. and Strauss, B. (2000) *Millennials Rising: The Next Generation*. New York, NY: Vintage Press.

Hughes, P. (2007) *Putting Life Together: Findings from Australian Youth Spirituality Research*. Fairfield, VIC: Fairfield Press.

Humanist Philosophers' Group (2001) *Religious Schools: The Case Against*. London: British Humanist Association.

Husserl, E. (1965) (trans. Q. Laver) *Phenomenology and the Crisis of Philosophy*. New York, NY: Harper Torchbooks.

Husserl, E. (1976) *Ideas: General Introduction to Pure Phenomenology* (trans. W. Gibson). New York, NY: Humanities Press.

Hyde, B. (2003a) 'Spiritual intelligence: A critique.' *Journal of Religious Education 51*, 1, 13–20.

Hyde, B. (2003b) 'Lifeworld existentials: Guides to reflection on a child's spirituality.' *Journal of Religious Education 51*, 3, 27–33.

Hyde, B. (2004a) 'The plausibility of spiritual intelligence: Spiritual experience, problem solving, and neural sites.' *International Journal of Children's Spirituality 9*, 1, 39–52.

Hyde, B. (2004b) 'Children's Spirituality and "The Good Shepherd Experience".' *Religious Education 99*, 2, 137–150.

Hyde, B. (2004c) 'A pedagogy of the spirit: Situating primary religious education within the greater ambit of spirituality.' *Journal of Religious Education 52*, 33, 69–76.

Hyde, B. (2005) 'Beyond logic – entering the realm of mystery: Hermeneutic phenomenology as a tool for reflecting on children's spirituality.' *International Journal of Children's Spirituality 10*, 1, 31–44.

Hyde, B. (2006a) 'You can't buy love: Trivializing and the challenge for religious education.' *Journal of Beliefs and Values 27*, 2, 165–176.

Hyde, B. (2006b) 'Nurturing the Spirit in Primary Religious Education Classrooms.' In M. de Souza, G. Durka, K. Engebretson, R. Jackson and A. McGrady (eds) *International Handbook of the Religious, Moral and Spiritual Dimensions in Education*. Dordrecht, The Netherlands: Springer.

James, W. (1977) *The Varieties of Religious Experience: A Study in Human Nature.* London: Fountain Books.

Kessler, R. (2000) *The Soul of Education: Helping Students Find Connection, Compassion and Character.* Alexandria: Association for Supervision and Curriculum Development.

Kibble, D. (2003) 'Sailing between Ofsted, Scylla and Charybdis: A Yorkshire school gives new meaning to spiritual development.' *International Journal of Children's Spirituality 8,* 1, 33–41.

Kohn, R. (1996) 'Cults and the New Age in Australia.' In G. Bouma (ed.) *Many Religions, All Australian: Religious Settlement, Identity and Cultural Diversity.* Kew, VIC: Christian Research Association.

Krathwohl, D., Bloom, B. and Masia, B. (1964) *Taxonomy of Educational Objectives. The Classification of Educational Goals. Book 2: Affective Domain.* London: Longman.

Kvale, S. (1996) *InterViews: An Introduction to Qualitative Research Interviewing.* Thousand Oaks, CA: Sage.

Kwilecki, S. (2000) 'Spiritual intelligence as a theory of individual religion: A case application.' *International Journal for the Psychology of Religion 10,* 1, 35–46.

Lincoln, Y. and Guba, E. (1985) *Naturalistic Inquiry.* Beverley Hills, CA: Sage.

Maitra, S. (1968) *The Meeting of the East and the West in Sri Aurobindo's Philosophy.* Pondicherry: Sri Aurobindo Ashram.

Marples, R. (2005) 'Against faith schools: A philosophical argument for children's rights.' *International Journal of Children's Spirituality 10,* 2, 133–147.

Marshak, D. and Litfin, K. (2002) 'Aurobindo Ghose.' In J. Miller and Y. Nakagawa (eds) *Nurturing Our Wholeness: Perspectives on Spirituality in Education.* Rutland, VT: Foundation for Educational Renewal.

Maslow, A. (1970a) *Religions, Values, and Peak Experiences.* New York, NY: The Viking Press.

Maslow, A. (1970b) *Motivation and Personality* (2nd edn). New York, NY: Harper and Row.

Mayer, J. (2000) 'Spiritual intelligence or spiritual consciousness?' *International Journal for the Psychology of Religion 10,* 1, 47–56.

McCreery, E. (1996) 'Talking to Children about Things Spiritual.' In R. Best (ed.) *Education, Spirituality and the Whole Child.* London: Cassell.

Meehan, C. (2002) 'Confusion and competing claims in the spiritual development debate.' *International Journal of Children's Spirituality 7,* 3, 291–308.

Mercer, J. (2004) 'The child as consumer: A North American problem of ambivalence concerning the spirituality of childhood in late capitalist consumer culture.' A paper presented at the 5th International Conference on Children's Spirituality, Bishop Grosseteste College, Lincoln, UK.

Merleau-Ponty, M. (1996) *Phenomenology of Perception* (trans. C. Smith). London: Routledge.

Merleau-Ponty, M. (2004) *The World of Perception* (trans. O. Davis). London: Routledge.

Merton, T. (1978) *The New Man.* New York, NY: Farrar, Straus and Giroux.

Moffett, J. (1994) *The Universal Schoolhouse: Spiritual Awakening through Education.* San Francisco, CA: Jossey-Bass.

Mommaers, P. (2003) *The Riddle of Christian Mystical Experience: The Role of the Humanity of Jesus.* Louvain, Belgium: Peeters Press.

Moriarty, W. (2007) 'Children's experience of time, and how this impacts on their spirituality.' A paper presented at the 5th National Symposium on Religious Education and Ministry, Australian Catholic University, Brisbane, Australia.

Mountain, V. (2004) *Investigating the Meaning and Function of Prayer for Children in Selected Primary Schools in Melbourne, Australia.* Unpublished PhD thesis, Australian Catholic University, Melbourne, Australia.

National Curriculum Council (1993) *Spiritual and Moral Development: A Discussion Paper.* York: NCC.

Newberg, A., d'Aquili, E. and Rause, V. (2001) *Why God Won't Go Away: Brain Science and the Biology of Belief.* New York, NY: Ballantine.

Nye, R. and Hay, D. (1996) 'Identifying children's spirituality: Where do you start without a starting point?' *British Journal of Religious Education 18*, 145–156.

O'Connor, T. (1999) *Uluru* [CD recording]. Nambour, QLD: Studio Horizon.

Office for Standards in Education (1994) *Handbook for the Inspection of Schools.* London: Ofsted.

O'Murchu, D. (1997) *Reclaiming Spirituality: A New Spiritual Framework for Today's World.* Dublin: Gateway.

Ota, C. (2001) 'The Conflict between Pedagogical Effectiveness and Spiritual Development in Catholic Schools.' In J. Erricker, C. Ota and C. Erricker (eds) *Spiritual Education. Cultural, Religious and Social Differences: New Perspectives for the 21st Century.* Brighton: Sussex Academic.

Palmer, S. (2007) *Toxic Childhood: How The Modern World is Damaging our Children and What We Can Do About It.* London: Orion.

Persinger, M. (1996) 'Feelings of past lives as expected perturbations within the neurocognitive processes that generate the sense of self: Contributions from limbic lability and vectoral hemisphericity.' *Perceptual and Motor Skills 83*, 3, 1107–1121.

Phillips, S. (2006) 'The Theatre of Learning: Developing Spirituality through Experiential and Active Techniques which also Promote Academic Achievement in Religious Education.' In M. de Souza, K. Engebretson, G. Durka, R. Jackson and A. McGrady (eds) *International Handbook of the Religious, Moral and Spiritual Dimensions in Education.* Dordrecht, The Netherlands: Springer.

Priestley, J. (2002) 'The spiritual dimension of the curriculum: Can it be assessed?' A paper presented at the 3rd International Conference on Children's Spirituality, King Alfred's College, Winchester, UK.

Ramachandran, V. and Blakeslee, S. (1998) *Phantoms of the Brain: Probing the Mysteries of the Human Mind.* London: Fourth Estate.

Ranson, D. (2002) *Across the Great Divide: Bridging Spirituality and Religion Today.* Strathfield, NSW: St. Paul's.

Reimer, K. and Furrow, J. (2001) 'A qualitative exploration of relational consciousness in Christian children.' *International Journal of Children's Spirituality 6*, 1, 7–23.

Robinson, E. (1977) *The Original Vision: A Study of the Religious Experience of Childhood.* Manchester College, Oxford: The Religious Experience Research Unit.

Rolheiser, R. (1998) *Seeking Spirituality: Guidelines for a Christian Spirituality for the Twenty-first Century.* London: Hodder and Stoughton.

Rossiter, G. (2005) 'From St. Ignatius to Obi-Wan Kenobi: An evaluative perspective on spirituality for school education.' *Journal of Religious Education 53*, 1, 3–22.

Schwandt, T. (1994) 'Constructivist, Interpretivist Approaches to Human Inquiry.' In N. Denzin and Y. Lincoln (eds) *Handbook of Qualitative Research*. Thousand Oaks, CA: Sage.

Scott, D. (2001) 'Storytelling, Voice and Qualitative Research: Spirituality as a Site of Ambiguity and Difficulty.' In J. Erricker, C. Ota and C. Erricker (eds) *Spiritual Education. Cultural, Religious and Social Differences: New Perspectives for the 21st Century*. Brighton: Sussex Academic.

Scott, D. (2004) 'Retrospective spiritual narratives: Exploring recalled childhood and adolescent spiritual experiences.' *International Journal of Children's Spirituality 9*, 1, 67–79.

Shannon, W. (2003) 'Thomas Merton in Dialogue with Eastern Traditions.' In P. O'Connell (ed.) *The Vision of Thomas Merton*. Notre Dame, IN: Ave Maria.

Sharkey, P. (2001) 'Hermeneutic Phenomenology.' In R. Barnacle (ed.) *Phenomenology: Qualitative Research Methods*. Melbourne: RMIT University Press.

Sinetar, M. (2000) *Spiritual Intelligence: What We can Learn from the Early Awakening Child*. New York, NY: Orbis.

Stearns, P. (2001) *Consumerism in World History: The Global Transformation of Desire*. London: Routledge.

St. John of the Cross (1542–1591) *Stanzas Between the Soul and the Bridegroom (The Whole Canticle)*. Grand Rapids, MI: Classics Ethereal Library. Accessed June 27, 2005, at www.ccel.org/john_cross/canticle.hmtl

St Teresa of Jesus (1577) *The Interior Castle*. ICS Publications. Accessed 20 October 2004 at www.carmelite.com/PDF/ic.pdf

Tacey, D. (2000) *ReEnchantment: The New Australian Spirituality*. Sydney, NSW: HarperCollins.

Tacey, D. (2003) *The Spirituality Revolution: The Emergence of Contemporary Spirituality*. Sydney, NSW: HarperCollins.

Thatcher, A. (1996) '"Policing the Sublime": A Wholly (holy?) Ironic Approach to the Spiritual Development of Children.' In J. Astley and L. Francis (eds) *Christian Theology and Religious Education: Connections and Contradictions*. London: SPCK.

Thatcher, A. (1999) 'Theology, Spirituality and the Curriculum – An Overview.' In A. Thatcher (ed.) *Spirituality and the Curriculum*. London: Cassell.

Thomas, T. (2001) 'Moments out of time: A family canoes the north woods.' *International Journal of Children's Spirituality 6*, 1, 85–98.

van Manen, M. (1990) *Researching Lived Experience: Human Science for an Action Sensitive Pedagogy*. London, Ontario: Althouse.

Watson, J. (2003) 'Preparing spirituality for citizenship.' *International Journal of Children's Spirituality 8*, 1, 9–24.

Webster, S. (2004) 'An existential framework of spirituality.' *International Journal of Children's Spirituality 9*, 1, 7–19.

Weinsheimer, J. (1985) *Gadamer's Hermeneutics: A Reading of Truth and Method*. New Haven, CT: Yale University Press.

Wilber, K. (2000a) 'Waves, Streams, States and Self: Further Considerations for an Integral Theory of Consciousness.' In J. Andresen and R. Forman (eds) *Cognitive Models and Spiritual Maps: Interdisciplinary Explorations of Religious Experience*. Thorverton: Imprint Academic.

Wilber, K. (2000b) *Integral Psychology: Consciousness, Spirit, Psychology.* London: Shambhala.

Wild, M. (1993) *Toby.* Norwood, South Australia: Omnibus.

Wright, A. (2000) 'The Spiritual Education Project: Cultivating Spiritual and Religious Literacy through a Critical Pedagogy of Religious Education.' In M. Grimmitt (ed.) *Pedagogies of Religious Education: Case Studies in the Research and Development of Good Pedagogic Practice in RE.* Great Wakering: McCrimmon.

Wright, A. (2004) *Religion, Education and Post-modernity.* London: RoutledgeFalmer.

Zohar, D. and Marshall, I. (2000) *SQ Spiritual Intelligence: The Ultimate Intelligence.* London: Bloomsbury.

Subject Index

Author Index